HEROES OF RACING

TONY STEWART

Rocket on the Racetrack

by Ryan Basen

Enslow Publishers, Inc.
40 Industrial Road
Box 398
Berkeley Heights, NJ 07922
USA
http://www.enslow.com

Library of Congress Cataloging-in-Publication Data
Basen, Ryan.
Tony Stewart : rocket on the racetrack / Ryan Basen.
p. cm. — (Heroes of racing)
Includes bibliographical references and index.
Summary: "A biography of NASCAR sports star Tony Stewart"—Provided by publisher.
ISBN-13: 978-0-7660-2998-9
ISBN-10: 0-7660-2998-0
1. Stewart, Tony, 1971—Juvenile literature. 2. Automobile racing drivers—United States—Biography—Juvenile literature. I. Title.
GV1032.S743B37 2008
796.72092—dc22
[B]
2007016073

Credits
Editorial Direction: Red Line Editorial (Bob Temple)
Editor: Sue Green
Designer: Becky Daum

Printed in the United States of America

10 9 8 7 6 5 4 3 2 1

To Our Readers: We have done our best to make sure all Internet addresses in this book were active and appropriate when we went to press. However, the author and the publisher have no control over and assume no liability for the material available on those Internet sites or on other Web sites they may link to. Any comments or suggestions can be sent by e-mail to comments@enslow.com or to the address on the back cover.

Photo credits: Ric Feld/AP Images, 1; Darron Cummings/AP Images, 4; Tom Strattman/AP Images, 8, 16; Richard Drew/AP Images, 13; Chuck Burton/AP Images, 25, 93; AP Images, 29; Mike Fiala/AP Images, 38; Craig Williby/AP Images, 40; Jim Topper/AP Images, 42; Terry Renna/AP Images, 44; Tim Boyd/AP Images, 50; J. Pat Carter/AP Images, 53; David Graham/AP Images, 58-59; Janet Hostetter/AP Images, 68; Evan Vucci/AP Images, 75; Mansfield News Journal, Jason J. Molyet/AP Images, 78; Glenn Smith/AP Images, 86-87; Jim Cole/AP Images, 89; Al Behrman/AP Images, 96; Mike McCarn/AP Images, 103; Matt Slocum/AP Images, 104; Robert E. Klein/AP Images, 111

Cover Photo: Ric Feld/AP Images

CONTENTS

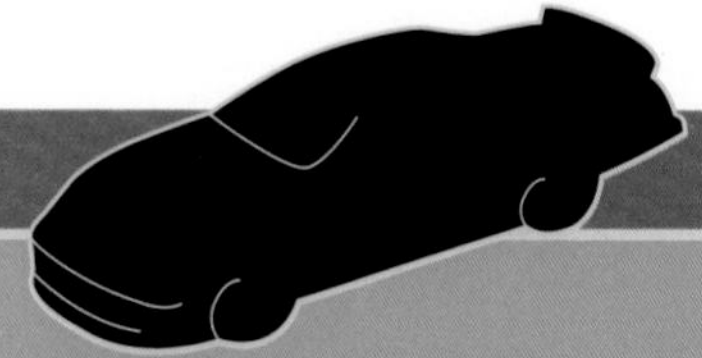

NEXTEL
HOME
DEPOT

1 A SPECTACULAR SEASON

On a typically hot August afternoon, thousands of people inside the Indianapolis Motor Speedway applauded and gazed at the track below them. Although they had come to watch dozens of different men race stock cars, now that the race had ended, most of their eyes and attention were focused on one man.

That man, Tony Stewart, cried tears of joy—and kissed a pile of bricks.

Tony Stewart hoists the trophy after winning the Allstate 400 at the Brickyard at the Indianapolis Motor Speedway in 2005.

TONY STEWART FILE

Height: 5-feet-9
Weight: 180 pounds
Born: May 20, 1971
Car: No. 20
Sponsor: The Home Depot
Manufacturer: Toyota
Team: Joe Gibbs Racing

NOTES: Grew up in Columbus, Indiana, 45 miles (72 kilometers) south of Indianapolis; started racing competitively at age eight

This scene was not too surprising. It was not unusual for Stewart to show emotion. He had developed a reputation on the NASCAR circuit as a hothead, somebody who reacted angrily to questionable moves by other drivers and said what was on his mind without always thinking first.

But this moment on August 7, 2005, was different. Stewart, an Indiana native, had just won the Allstate 400 in Indianapolis, the state capital. He had captured his first NASCAR Cup race in his home state, and he did it at the famed Indianapolis Motor Speedway. In doing so, he had fulfilled a childhood dream.

"There's so much pressure that I put on myself to do good here just because of the history of the place and being so close and growing up around it," he said later. "If I died right now, my life's complete."[1]

A JOYOUS OCCASION

Many people in the stands understood how Stewart felt. So, just after Stewart held off forty-two challengers to win the NASCAR Nextel Cup race, most of the crowd of 250,000—including Stewart's father, mother, sister, and friends—stood and cheered. Other drivers who had just lost to Stewart congratulated him. Reporters and television analysts praised him.

Stewart responded by taking three victory laps, thanking his crew, crawling out of his Home Depot No. 20 Chevrolet, and climbing a fence that separated the track from the fans to salute them. After he let himself down, he rode around the track in a pace car to acknowledge the adoring fans some more.

Then he got out of the car and walked toward the track's most famous landmark—the wall of bricks. With members of his crew and family beside him, Stewart kneeled, bent over, and planted several kisses on the bricks.

"This is one of those days that I don't want to end," he said later. "It's definitely the greatest day of my life up to this point.

"After years of trying to win (at Indianapolis), be it in Indy cars or stock cars, I got to know what it feels like, to see that view coming down the front straightaway, seeing the checkered flag. I had wanted that moment for so long, and I finally got it."[2]

Tony Stewart kisses the bricks on the finish line after winning the 2005 Allstate 400 at the Brickyard.

A PLACE IN HISTORY

The Allstate 400 was an important victory for Stewart personally. It was also one of several that he posted during an outstanding 2005 Nextel Cup season.

Stewart won five of seven races during a dominant midseason stretch, including his performance in Indianapolis. After winning that race, Stewart went on to win another one in Watkins Glen, New York, the following week and placed second in three more races in September and October. That helped him build a huge lead in the series points standings.

When Stewart placed in the top fifteen in the season's final race, the Ford 400 in Miami, he clinched the series title. That, combined with his first Cup title in 2002, gave Stewart two Cup titles in his short

NASCAR career. He is one of only fifteen drivers in history to win multiple Cup titles. The trio of Stewart, Jeff Gordon and Jimmie Johnson are the only active drivers among that number.

"To be in a group where there's only 14 of us in the past 50 years or so that have won more than once is a huge, huge honor," Stewart said.[3]

That honor was significant. It meant that by the end of 2005 Stewart had become one of the elite drivers in NASCAR. He is in select company and has accomplished feats that nobody else in the history of American professional stock car racing has.

Besides winning the two NASCAR Cup championships, Stewart has also won go-kart national titles, an Indy car title, and captured the United States Auto Club's (USAC) Triple Crown by winning titles in National Midget, Sprint, and Silver Crown divisions. He is also one of only nine drivers in history to win races in all three NASCAR premier series—Nextel Cup, Busch, and Craftsman Truck.

In short, Tony Stewart is a winner.

"He is the greatest driver I've seen in this era," said fellow NASCAR driver Mark Martin.[4]

DID YOU KNOW?

From 1999 to 2005, Stewart earned twenty-four wins. That was the second-most victories of any driver during that span. Only Jeff Gordon earned more wins.

STEWART'S CAREER

1986-1995:
Raced go-karts in Indiana and in national competitions such as races on the World Karting Association circuit

1989-1995:
Raced various cars in the United States Auto Club circuit

1995-1998:
Raced Indy cars, mostly in the Indy Racing League

1998:
Raced Indy cars and stock cars in a minor NASCAR series and in the NASCAR Busch series

1999-2001:
Raced in NASCAR's Winston Cup series, also raced Indy cars

2001-present:
Races in NASCAR's Winston/Nextel Cup series

Winning so much has helped make Stewart one of the most popular NASCAR drivers around. So has his love of racing. He will race any car, any time, anywhere. He even has arrived unannounced at random dirt tracks throughout the United States and raced under fake names.

"I'm a racecar driver," Stewart said. "That's what I do."[5]

A STRONG PERSONALITY

But Stewart is about a lot more than racing. He is a deep, controversial figure. He often gets into scraps with fellow drivers and has feuded with members of the media. He nearly had his booming career cut short when his temper almost cost him his Home Depot sponsorship and his race team a few years ago.

He wants to be honest with the media, sponsors, and race fans, he says, although he knows an honest answer may anger a lot of them.

Stewart is "one of the sport's most passionate drivers and the undisputed king of NASCAR controversy," wrote a *USA Today* columnist in 2005.[6]

"Tony's an intense competitor who's very focused on driving," said Joe Gibbs, who used to direct Joe Gibbs Racing, the team for which Stewart races. "During or around the race weekend, he wears his emotions on his sleeve. He can get caught up and step over the line in some of those cases. That's why he's a little different."[7]

But Stewart is also known as a generous, grounded person. He has a successful foundation that assists underprivileged children, gives a lot of his time and money to other charities and good causes, and loves to spend time with close friends and family.

These contradictions in his personality, in addition to his success on the track, are what make Stewart such an interesting driver.

"He's cool. I like Tony a lot," said fellow driver Dale Earnhardt, Jr. "I like his attitude. The guy just

DID YOU KNOW?

The pseudonyms, or fake names, that Stewart races under at small dirt tracks include Smoke Johnson and Luke Warmwater.

DID YOU KNOW?

Stewart hosts a radio show on Sirius Satellite Radio every Tuesday night with racing reporter Matt Yocum.

wants to be himself. He doesn't really care whether you like it or not."[8]

"He's one of the best racecar drivers I've ever raced against," fellow driver Jeff Gordon said. "The only thing Tony has going against him is he's got a bit of a temper, and sometimes that gets the best of him.

"Off the track, he certainly keeps us entertained. He's a great guy and a very gracious person, but sometimes little things set him off."[9]

The little things do not set Stewart off as much as they used to, though. He has grown up a lot since he started racing in NASCAR's top series in 1999.

By the time he had capped 2005, his seventh full NASCAR season, with a second championship, he had impressed teammates, reporters, fellow drivers, and others by how far he had come.

Many of them recalled his win in Indianapolis. The image of Stewart weeping, grinning, and kissing the bricks at the Allstate 400 was the defining moment of the 2005 season for many race fans and insiders.

"Seeing that smile on his face will be a vision burned in there forever," said Greg Zipadelli, Stewart's crew chief.[10]

The moment was vintage Stewart: winning, showing emotion, and celebrating with those who are close to him. After he wrapped up the Nextel Cup title three months later, the young hotshot and his fans were excited about the possibilities that could come for Stewart in 2006—and beyond.

Tony Stewart poses with the Nextel Cup trophy during an appearance on "Today" in New York City.

2 GROWING UP

Nelson Stewart and his six-year-old son, Tony, arose early one morning in May 1977 at their southern Indiana home. They got dressed, left the house, and boarded a bus bound for Indianapolis.

It was early when the Stewarts got onto the bus, so a tired Tony climbed up into a luggage rack above the seat and tried to get some more sleep. Other people on the bus saw the boy and threw blankets on top of him to make him more comfortable.

The trip was worth the discomfort, though. When the Stewarts arrived at their destination, young Tony walked into the Indianapolis Motor Speedway for the first time. He was immediately awed by all of the action inside one of racing's most revered venues. The amazing speed at which the cars zipped by and the sounds and smells they made especially thrilled young Tony.

"We sat in Turns 3 and 4. We were two rows up, right in the middle of the short chute," he recalled years later. "The hard thing was you could hardly see anything. The cars were so fast. They were a blur.

"But to see those cars under caution and smell the methanol fumes and everything, it was still pretty cool."[1]

Nelson Stewart knew then that his son was destined to be a racecar driver.

"I remember, he was so mesmerized by the cars," Nelson said. "He couldn't take his eyes off them."[2]

He still has not taken his eyes off of racecars.

A DESIRE TO WIN

Tony grew up in Columbus, a small town about 45 miles (72 kilometers) south of Indianapolis. He was the older of two children. Tony liked to ride a toy motorcycle and Big Wheel around his back yard. He also would sometimes put a mixing bowl on his head as a helmet and ride a vacuum cleaner around the house, pretending to be a professional racecar driver.

Tony Stewart leads the field early in the 1997 Indy 500.

Tony helped his family pick corn, tomatoes, and other fruits and vegetables from a garden in their yard. His prime interest, though, was racing.

Recognizing his son's interest, Nelson entered Tony in local go-kart races when he was seven years old. Nelson served as Tony's first crew chief and car owner. He was demanding, pushing Tony to try his hardest and never quit. That approach helped make Tony into the successful driver he is today. It instilled in him a fierce competitiveness and a deep desire to win.

"He never let me settle for second," Tony said of his father. "He didn't like it when we ran second, and he knew that I didn't like it when we ran second. If he saw that I wasn't giving 100 percent, then he was on me pretty hard about it. He pushed me to be better.

"He never pressured me to be the best racecar driver in the world, but he did pressure me to be the best racecar driver that I could be. He never compared me to anybody else. He expected that what I could do was what I could do.

"That's probably why you see so much fire in me today."[3]

As soon as he started racing, Tony displayed the racing style that he uses today. He went fast without fearing the consequences, took reckless turns, and raced on any type of track in any kind of vehicle.

COLUMBUS, INDIANA

Population: 39,000

Location: 45 miles (72 km) south of Indianapolis, sitting on a fork of the White River

Known for: Having great architecture, art, and parks

Famous natives: Besides Tony Stewart, Columbus has another famous native—Chuck Taylor, who designed the Chuck Taylor All-Star basketball sneakers that were popular in the 1950s.

He would do anything to be able to race—such as arm wrestle his car owner one day as a teenager. That owner did not want him to race in a certain event because the event would did not count in the standings. But Tony wanted to race, so he challenged the older man. Tony won two of three arm-wrestling matches. The owner promptly let him race.

Young Tony exhibited a love of racing—and a hatred of losing races.

"Whenever he lost a race as a kid and got upset you had to take him to get a hotdog to get him out of it," said Kurt Meyer, a family friend who helped Nelson Stewart buy Tony's first go-kart.[4]

"When I started racing," Tony said, "getting a trophy that was bigger than the other kids was all I cared about."[5]

Tony got a lot of those trophies. He won his first championship at age eight, when he captured a local karting title at the Columbus (Indiana) Fairgrounds in 1980. He won the International Karting Federation

DID YOU KNOW?

Tony Stewart's first racing title was a four-cycle rookie junior class karting championship, which he won as an eight-year-old at a Columbus (Indiana) Fairgrounds event in 1980. He later won the International Karting Federation Grand National championship in 1983 and the World Karting Association national championship in 1987.

Grand National championship in 1983 and the World Karting Association national championship in 1987.

EARNING A REPUTATION

By the time he was a teenager, Tony was well known in southern Indiana because of his racing success. He raced so fast and so well that he earned a nickname: The Rushville Rocket, after another nearby town in Indiana.

The Stewarts made Tony's races a family event. Nelson would work with Tony to prepare for the races, and then help him if anything went wrong during the events. Pam Boas, Tony's mother, volunteered to keep track of the scoring and race times. Tony's younger sister Natalie was the runner between the pits and the tower.

"Even though it was a bit unnerving, I became very involved," Boas recalled. "We did that every Saturday night for 10 years. We were always grateful when it came time to take a break because we didn't take vacations until the racing season was over. But it was nothing that I would ever regret."[6]

As a teenager, Tony sometimes drove a tow truck in Indianapolis and cleaned windows at a local car wash to raise money for racing. He spent his free time shooting pool, eating at local restaurants with his friends, wrestling with his father, and playing the trombone in his high school band.

A.J. FOYT FILE

Professional driver from 1953 to 1994

Highlights: Won the Indianapolis 500 four times, the Daytona 500, and the 24 Hours of LeMans; raced in the Indianapolis 500 each year from 1957 to 1992; inducted into Motorsports Hall of Fame in 1989

From: Houston, Texas

Born: January 16, 1935

Lives: Hockley, Texas, near Houston

"I'm just a simple boy from Indiana," Tony said. "I don't want to be a legend or an icon or anything. I just want to be a racecar driver, pure and simple."[7]

While growing up in Indiana, Tony watched a lot of professional races on television and in person. He looked up to A.J. Foyt, who won the Daytona 500 and the Indianapolis 500 four times while racing professionally for nearly four decades. Tony's favorite race was—and still is—the Indianapolis 500.

"I never missed an Indy 500 race, whether it was (at the track) or on TV," Tony said. "I don't think, growing up in Indiana, anybody missed it."[8]

TAKING ON NEW CHALLENGES

By 1989, eighteen-year-old Tony was racing three-quarter midget cars, which have much more horsepower than karts and are open-wheel vehicles.

That made them more difficult to race. But Tony could handle the new challenge.

Crocky Wright, a racing enthusiast who lives in Indianapolis, recalled watching Tony race midget cars one day at a track in Madison, Indiana.

"The first time I saw him warm up a car, I thought he would be special," said Wright, a former dirt-track driver.[9]

He was special. Tony dominated the midget races, just as he had conquered the go-kart races. By the time he hit his late teens, he was ready for a new challenge. It was soon time for him to leave the comforts of home in Indiana and take his talents to a much bigger stage.

THE INDIANAPOLIS 500

An annual Indy Car race held every Memorial Day weekend

Laps: **200**

Distance: **500 miles (805 km)**

Where: **Indianapolis Motor Speedway**

The first race: **1911**

Top winners: **A.J. Foyt, Al Unser, and Rick Mears had each won the race four times**

3 BECOMING A PROFESSIONAL DRIVER

One day late in 1997, a nervous Tony Stewart looked at Joe Gibbs, took a pen, and signed a contract to race stock cars in a NASCAR series.

Stewart was thrilled. He would soon be joining some of the most popular, successful drivers in the United States to compete in one of the fastest-growing sports in the world. And he would be competing for the legendary owner of Joe Gibbs Racing.

"I'm excited," Stewart said. "This is going to be a fun ride."[1]

Within a year, Stewart would be racing in NASCAR's Winston Cup series. Joining that series, NASCAR's top circuit, would be the culmination of a lifetime of racing and a decade of hard work as a professional driver.

Stewart had begun racing go-karts as a kid in southern Indiana, and then moved on to three-quarter midget cars as a teenager. He had a lot of success in both.

Soon after graduating from Columbus North High School, Stewart decided to become a professional driver. He signed a contract to race midget cars for a local car owner and competed in several divisions of the United States Auto Club (USAC) series, which were held all across the country.

JOE GIBBS RACING

Formed: In 1991 by Joe Gibbs and Don Meredith

First driver: Dale Jarrett

Owner: Joe Gibbs

President: J.D. Gibbs

Stats: Gibbs' drivers had won fifty-eight NASCAR Nextel/Winston Cup races and three series titles as of the end of the 2007 season.

Sponsors: Interstate Batteries, The Home Depot

The young driver continued to have success and began to earn some money and regional attention for his prowess. He was the USAC's Rookie of the Year in 1991 and earned a reputation as a driver who would show up to race any type of vehicle, anywhere. He ran in about sixty-five races annually on short tracks.

"If I could race seven days a week," Stewart said, "I'd race seven days a week."[2]

PROVING HIMSELF A CHAMPION

It was not long before Stewart won professional championships—in different USAC circuits. He secured the National Midget championship in 1994, winning three of the first six races in that series. He placed second in the other three races to start the season and won five of twenty-two overall.

The next year Stewart ran 106 races altogether and won the USAC's Triple Crown. He captured titles in three national open-wheel series: the National Midget, Silver Crown, and Sprint. He was the first driver ever to do so.

"I think this ranks as one of the major accomplishments in the history of the sport," said Dick Jordan, of the USAC. "I cannot explain to people how significant this is."[3]

Stewart placed second in his first Indy car race, in Orlando, Florida, despite having little time for practice runs. That drew praise from Menard.

"To bring a rookie to a very demanding track, with very little coaching, and have him do so well is very gratifying," Menard said.[4]

Stewart raced so often that he spent only six days at home in four months during the height of racing season. His success and love of racing had fans and race promoters calling him the "next Jeff Gordon," after the fellow Indiana native who was the same age as Stewart. Gordon at the time was starting to light up NASCAR's Winston Cup series.

"Everything has sort of happened at once," Stewart said in 1996. "A year ago, no one recognized me anywhere and we ran more races than anyone except maybe a World of Outlaws driver."[5]

JEFF GORDON FILE

Born: August 4, 1971

Grew up:
Vallejo, California, and Pittsboro, Indiana

Background: Won USAC national championships in sprint cars

Racing highlights: Won four Winston/Nextel Cup series titles through 2006 season and won three Daytona 500 races

Car: No. 24

Manufacturer: Chevrolet

Sponsor: DuPont

Team:
Hendrick Motorsports

Stewart "is just what Indianapolis Motor Speedway president Tony George had in mind when he created the Indy Racing League," a newspaper columnist wrote in May 1996. "No special favors—nothing but seat time and hard work—got him the ride he has."[6]

Joe Gibbs watches a qualifying race with his grandson, Jackson.

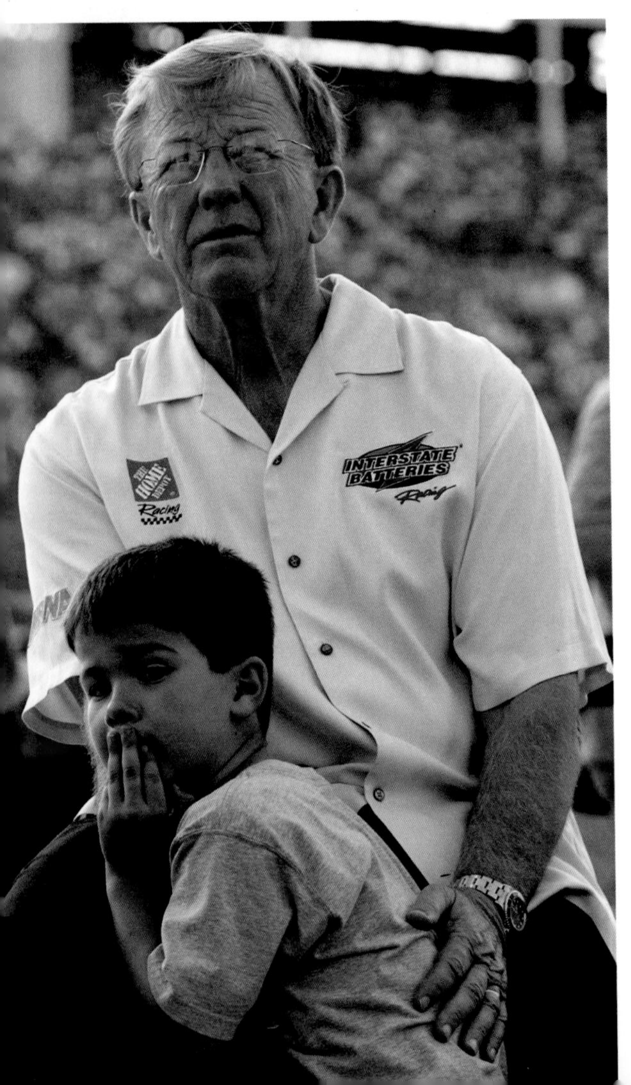

A DREAM TURNS INTO A NIGHTMARE

In 1996, Stewart for the first time qualified to race in his favorite event: the Indianapolis 500. Not only that, but he qualified second. He was just behind teammate Scott Bray-ton, the pole sitter.

The two were good friends and fierce competitors. They looked forward to racing from the top two spots in their first Indy 500 together.

STEWART'S 1996 INDY RACING LEAGUE SEASON

Races: Three

Best finish: Second at Walt Disney World Speedway, January 27

Notable:
Three top-twelve finishes

For Stewart, then twenty-five years old, Memorial Day Weekend of 1996 was shaping up to be one of the best weekends of his life. He would be racing in front of friends and family. Fans and promoters would be closely following his progress. A big day could mean big money and national fame, as well as admiration and support from those closest to him.

"He's the total package, a promoter's dream: He is 25, handsome, articulate, cocky, and can flat-out drive a racecar," a newspaper columnist wrote just before the race.[7]

Stewart was excited for the race. He would be competing on the track that had drawn him into racing on that day when he watched his first Indy 500 as a six-year-old. He kept a sleeping bag in a crawl space above his team's garage in the month leading up to the race, so he could spend as much time at the track as possible.

SCOTT BRAYTON FILE

- **Qualified for fourteen consecutive Indianapolis 500 races, running in thirteen**
- **Raced for John Menard from 1994 to 1996**
- **Died practicing for 1996 Indy 500 on May 17, 1996, at age thirty-seven**

THE 1996 INDIANAPOLIS 500

Winner: **Buddy Lazier**

Winning time: **3 hours, 22 minutes, 45.8 seconds**

Tony Stewart's finish: **Twenty-fourth, eighty-two laps with a Lola/Menard V6 engine**

"My goal has always been to become a professional driver," Stewart said. "I've given up everything in my personal life to be here. This is where I wanted to be. I've reached my goal. I'm at Indianapolis and racing at the biggest event in the world."[8]

Stewart's first Indy 500 as a driver would prove to be a disaster, however.

Just a week before the race, Brayton was conducting a practice run when he blew a tire going into Turn 2. He crashed his backup car into the outside retaining wall in the track's south end.

Brayton died almost instantly. Stewart was emotionally crushed.

"I've been through a lot of things this month normal people only go through in the course of a lifetime, as far as emotions," Stewart said shortly after Brayton's death. "I guess in a way it makes you grow up to understand what happens, how to deal with it and how to go on. Dealing with Scott's accident, it's a big adjustment."[9]

A weary Stewart moved up to the top position for the race and placed a decal on his car reading: "FOR SCOTTY, WE LOVE YA!" But neither action helped him. Despite leading for the first thirty-one laps, he finished twenty-fourth in the race.

Scott Brayton died shortly after crashing during practice on May 17, 1996.

MOVING ON

It took a while for Stewart to get over Brayton's death and his disappointing Indy 500 finish. But he eventually

STEWART'S 1997 INDY RACING LEAGUE SEASON

Races: Ten

Best finish: Won at Pikes Peak International Raceway, June 29

Notable: Won series; finished second at Phoenix International Raceway on March 23

snapped out of his funk and got back to racing—and winning. Not even the death of a friend could stop such a committed driver.

"You can't let that bother you," Stewart said. "Nobody thinks like that. I'll always remember Scott Brayton, but if a race driver begins fearing what could happen, then it's time to get out."[10]

Stewart dominated the 1997 Indy Racing League. He earned his first IRL win at Pike's Peak in Colorado Springs, Colorado, in June 1997 and soon clinched the series championship. He led for 812 laps that season.

"He's one of the greatest young talents who have come along in oval racing," Team Menard manager Larry Curry said. "Tony has an unbelievable feel for racecars, and he has phenomenal skills in a race."[11]

By 1998, Stewart was attracting the attention of NASCAR team owners and officials. He preferred to race Indy cars. Stock cars did not appeal to him as much. Because of their larger size, he mockingly called them "taxi cabs." But he also appreciated that stock cars were more challenging to drive.

"If you're driving an Indy car at 220 miles per hour (354 kilometers per hour)," Stewart told a magazine writer, "then the aerodynamics are so good, you can pretty much floor it all the time. You're thinking about what you're going to have for dinner while you're sitting there."[12]

"Stock cars," the magazine wrote, "are heavier, 700-horse-power Neanderthals, custom-built throwback machines."[13]

"At the end of a straightaway," Stewart said, "you've got to use the brakes and force 3,400 pounds to change direction—which it doesn't want to do."[14]

NASCAR also drew the most interest from corporate sponsors, fans, and the media. Plus, it had the nation's most popular, successful drivers. For the ultra-competitive Stewart, racing in NASCAR was the most effective way for him to measure his driving skills.

STEWART'S 1998 INDY RACING LEAGUE SEASON

Races: Eleven

Best finish: Won at Walt Disney World Speedway on January 24; won at New Hampshire International Speedway on June 28

FINDING A MATCH IN NASCAR

By 1998, Stewart was "as smooth and as calculating as Rick Mears, and yet as versatile as A.J. Foyt," according to a magazine writer.[15] He was ready for NASCAR.

Stewart could not just sign with any NASCAR racing team, though. Some teams were put off by his emotional behavior. Others were too conservative for Stewart's tastes.

Then there was Joe Gibbs Racing. Gibbs, who had started the team in 1991, had previously been a successful head football coach with the NFL's Washington Redskins. In twelve years directing the Redskins, he often dealt well with such demonstrative players as defensive end Dexter Manley and wide receiver Gary Clark. Gibbs worked closely with them to get great results.

Similarly, Gibbs hoped to draw the best out of Stewart. Gibbs looked at working with Stewart as a potential challenge—not a headache. He was also attracted to Stewart's intense desire to win and his willingness to make sacrifices to be successful. So in 1997 Gibbs signed a short-term deal for

JOE GIBBS FILE

Team owner, Joe Gibbs Racing

Head coach, NFL's Washington Redskins (1981 to 1992, 2004 to present)

Pro Football Hall of Fame, 1996 inductee

STEWART'S 1998 NASCAR BUSCH SERIES SEASON

Races: Twenty-two

Top-five finishes: Five

Wins: Zero

Overall finish: Twenty-first

Stewart to run some races on the Busch Grand National circuit, a minor-league NASCAR series.

Stewart crashed in his first two Grand National races. But he placed third in a race in Charlotte in October 1997. That encouraged both Gibbs and Stewart.

"We're not surprised by what Tony did at Charlotte," Gibbs said. "We knew he was capable of being a fast learner."[16]

"The most important thing I learned out there (in Charlotte) was patience," Stewart said. "There were a lot of times on the restarts, I would pick the wrong line to go with and got shuffled to the back. It took some patience to get to the front.

"I'm so ecstatic I can't believe it. I couldn't believe it came together like it did for me."[17]

After watching Stewart run a few more Grand National races, Gibbs in 1998 offered him a three-year contract to drive for Joe Gibbs Racing. The plan was for Stewart to slowly work his way into competitive stock car racing. While continuing to race at the Indy 500, he would also compete in NASCAR's Busch series—one notch below the Winston Cup series.

Stewart was confident that he could make the transition to NASCAR.

"Everyone thinks I'm an Indy-car racer, but I'm not," Stewart said. "I'm a sprint car-midget racer that got an Indy-car ride. I really don't know very much about stock cars. But I'm learning pretty quick."[18]

Stewart went along with Gibbs' plan. He placed only thirty-first in his Busch series race debut in Daytona Beach, Fla. but he placed second in his next Busch race in Rockingham and finished in the top five of the twenty-two Busch races that he ran in 1998.

By the end of the year, Gibbs thought Stewart was ready for NASCAR's big-league circuit. Stewart, of course, was ready to go. He was excited about being a rookie on the Winston Cup circuit. But nobody—not Stewart, Gibbs, NASCAR drivers, or fans—was ready for the type of rookie season that Stewart would have.

"It's a new challenge for us," Stewart said, "and that's what motivates me."[19]

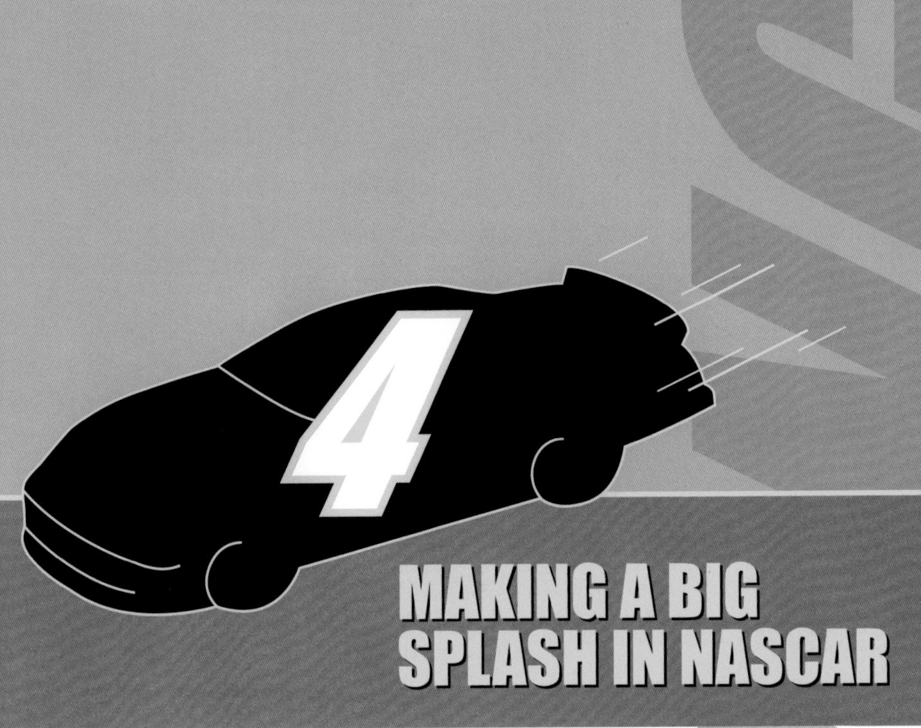

4 MAKING A BIG SPLASH IN NASCAR

Early in the afternoon on February 14, 1999, twenty-seven-year-old Tony Stewart climbed into an orange-and-black Pontiac with the number "20" and the words "Home Depot" inscribed in large type on both sides.

Stewart was preparing for his first official Winston Cup series race. It was the day of the Daytona 500, a popular annual NASCAR race held in Daytona Beach. He was a racing veteran, with many victories and other great driving achievements. But he was a Winston Cup series rookie, and he drove like it. Stewart led for none of the race's 200 laps and finished twenty-eighth. He learned an early lesson. The Winston Cup series has the best of the best drivers. He would have to drive at or near his best in order to compete.

He soon did.

ROOKIE EXPECTATIONS

The Daytona 500 was an exception to Stewart's 1999 season. He enjoyed an incredible rookie Winston Cup campaign—one of the most successful first-year seasons in NASCAR history.

Stewart became a NASCAR sensation almost overnight. He won many races and was competitive in others. He drew attention and fans because of his brash behavior, aggressive racing style, and a willingness to answer the media's questions honestly.

"Nobody in Winston Cup drove better than Tony Stewart in 1999," a reporter for *The Indianapolis Star* wrote just after the 1999 season ended. "No rookie ever shined like Stewart."[1]

Joe Gibbs, the owner of Stewart's team, had wanted to bring him along slowly. Gibbs' plan was for Stewart to use each race as a learning experience. Gibbs hoped that Stewart would qualify for and complete every race so that he could pick up the nuances of each track and each race. Then, in the 2000 season and beyond, he would ideally be able to use his new knowledge and begin to win races.

"We figured the more laps we could complete in every race, the more experience and track time I would get," Stewart said. "That would be more valuable than any testing we could do."[2]

With such modest goals, Stewart felt little pressure heading into his rookie campaign. He was even cautious on the eve of the season, as he prepared to race against some of the nation's best drivers.

"There's so much talent there that you can't expect to go in your rookie season and be successful," Stewart said. "I have to go into the '99 season with the attitude of learning as much as possible and just being consistent."[3]

That strategy was widely praised by NASCAR insiders. It was typical for rookie drivers to hang back and wait for their opportunities to come. That opportunity would typically arrive only after the rookie was familiar with the tracks and comfortable with the spotlight shown on Winston Cup drivers. Stewart, most people thought, would be no different.

"It's the freshmen who typically have the toughest time," one magazine

STEWART'S 1999 WINSTON CUP SEASON

Wins: Three

Top-five finishes: Twelve

Place: Fourth

Races not completed: One

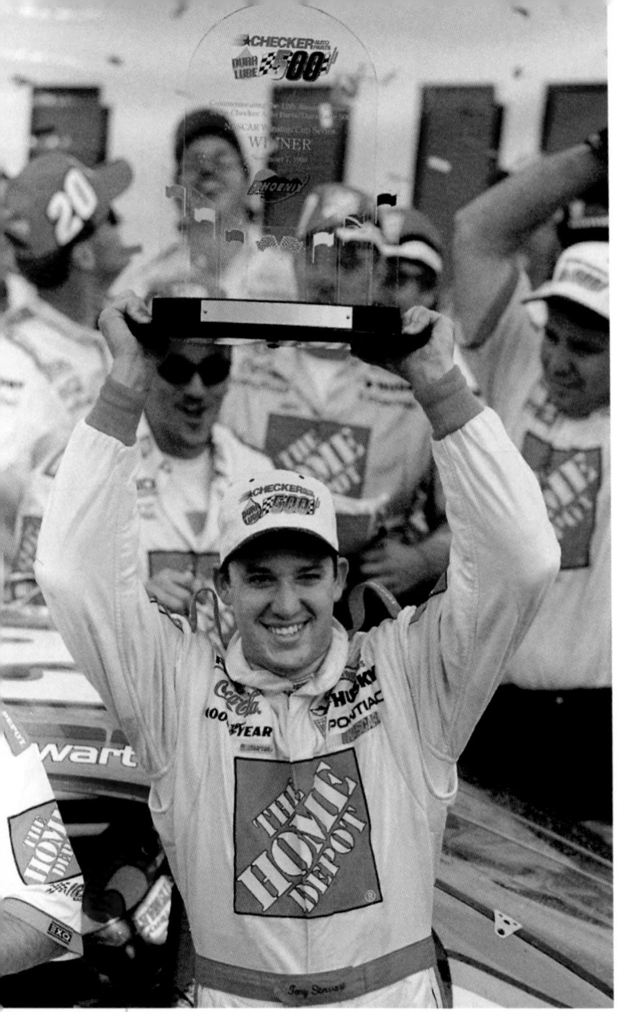

Tony Stewart hoists the trophy after a 1999 win in Arizona.

writer said. "They must learn new tracks, get comfortable in a new car, acclimate themselves to performing in front of the most vocal, passionate fans in sports, and compete against a group of racers not exactly known for driving with kid gloves. Survival, not winning, becomes the primary goal of the Winston Cup rookie."[4]

WINNING WAYS

But Stewart did much more than survive and learn. He exceeded the expectations of Gibbs, himself, and nearly everybody else in 1999. He won three Winston Cup races. He placed in the top five in a dozen races. After he won two straight races at the end of the season, at Phoenix International Raceway on November 7 and on November 14 at Homestead-Miami Speedway, Stewart clinched fourth place in the series.

"I knew he'd been successful in all types of racing, but I thought it would take him longer to adjust," veteran NASCAR driver Dale Jarrett said. "He had to show he could use his head, and he's done that."[5]

In 1999 Stewart completed all but one of the season's thirty-four races. During a six-month span, he finished in the top ten in eighteen of twenty-four races. When he won at Richmond (Virginia) International Raceway on September 11, he became the first rookie in twelve years to earn a victory on the Winston Cup circuit.

It was quite an enjoyable season for Stewart, who tried to cherish every moment of it.

"It's been a phenomenal year," Stewart said. "This is a job where if you fail there's always going to be 100 guys waiting in line to take your place. . . . So I just try to enjoy myself, (and) look for ways to make it fun."[6]

DID YOU KNOW?

By finishing fourth in 1999, Tony Stewart was the first rookie driver to place in the top ten of the Winston Cup circuit since Davey Allison in 1987. Stewart was the first rookie to place in the top five since James Hylton placed second in 1966.

Stewart drives his winning Pontiac across the finish line of the Kmart 400 race at Michigan Speedway.

Stewart benefited from that relaxed approach. He also was boosted by driving a polished car under the Gibbs team and by driving as a teammate of veteran Bobby Labonte. Amazingly, though, Stewart was working with a crew chief who was a rookie as well. The inexperience and lack of chemistry between Stewart and Greg Zipadelli somehow did not hold them back. "From (the first day) this race team came out of the box and acted like we worked with each other all our lives," Stewart said. "We've really got something special here."[7]

MAKING HISTORY

In 1999 Stewart made history in NASCAR and in the world of racing at large. In mid-season, he raced in both the Indianapolis 500 and Coca-Cola 600 on the same day, flying from Indianapolis to Charlotte between races. Stewart promptly placed in the top ten in both races, making him the first driver ever to accomplish such a feat.

"He's been pretty impressive," said fellow driver Richard Petty. "Right now, he's the one."[8]

While most racing insiders, such as Petty and Jarrett, were surprised by Stewart's rookie success, not everyone was. Those who had seen Stewart race before knew how competitive he was. They knew how much he loved to win and how good he was at winning.

"It doesn't surprise me at all," said Bob East, who owned the midget cars that Stewart drove to three different USAC championships in 1995. "This kid could go from winning the pole at Indy, jump in a midget with no hot laps, and win going away."[9]

Stewart's big rookie season carried into his sophomore year. Although he slipped a bit in the 2000 Winston Cup standings, finishing sixth, he won six series races. His season highlight came when he won races in consecutive weeks—on June 4 at Dover (Delaware) International Speedway and June 11 in Brooklyn, Michigan.

DID YOU KNOW?

Tony Stewart's first Winston Cup series win was at Richmond International Raceway on September 11, 1999. He became the first rookie to win a race since Davey Allison in 1987.

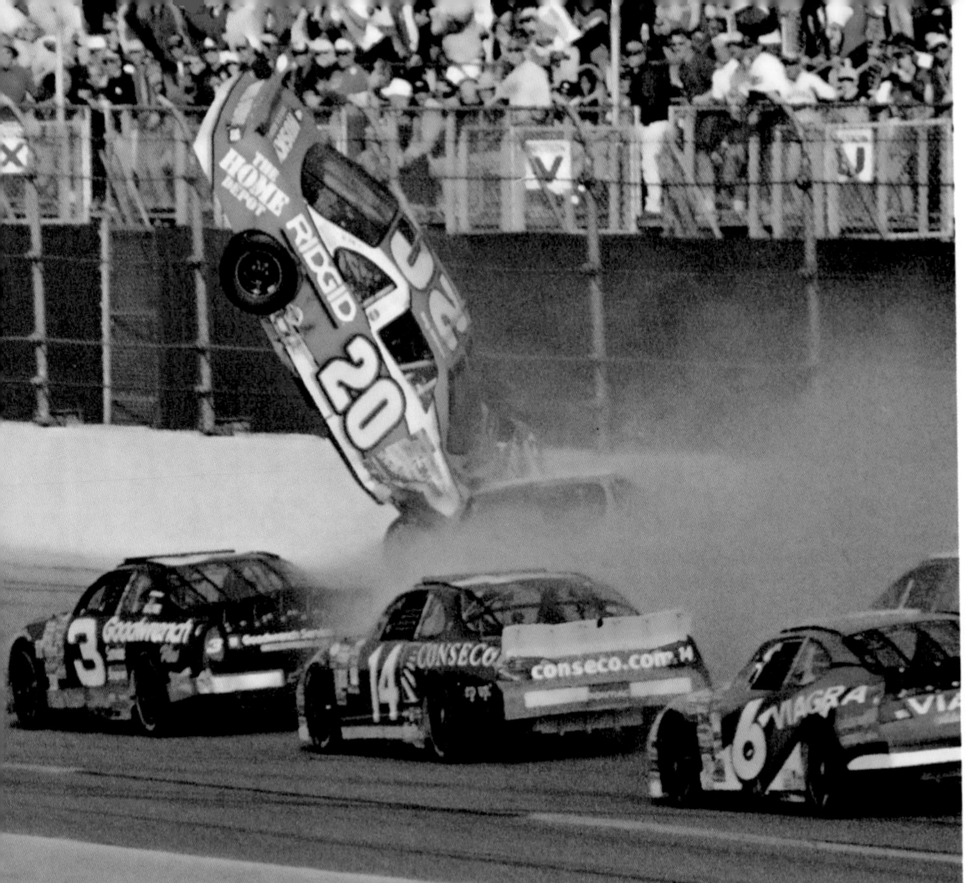

Stewart flies through the air during the 2001 Daytona 500.

STEWART'S 2000 WINSTON CUP SEASON

Wins: Six

Top-five finishes: Twelve

Races not completed: Five

Place: Sixth

Only five non-finishes, including four wrecks, prevented Stewart from placing in the top five and possibly winning the Winston Cup.

POISED FOR MORE SUCCESS

By 2001, his third season on the circuit, Stewart was one of the top drivers in the sport.

He was a threat to win any race and, despite his youth, did not defer to any of the veteran drivers he competed against. His aggressiveness and talent helped him rise to second in the series.

STEWART'S 2001 WINSTON CUP SEASON

Wins: Three

Top-five finishes: Fifteen

Races not completed: Four

Place: Second

Stewart started that season without much success. He was in eighteenth place after finishing twenty-fifth on March 25 at Bristol (Virginia) Motor Speedway. But he won three races after that. A late hot streak—he placed in the top ten in nine of ten races from late August to early November—helped Stewart make a late move.

By the end of the 2001 season, everything was set up for Stewart to take the next step and become a Winston Cup champion. He had always had the team, the owner, the car, and the talent to win a title. During three seasons, he gained the experience and savvy he would need.

Many observers thought Stewart could win it all the next year. None had any idea how hard it would be for him to do so.

NASCAR
Winston Cup
Series
JOE GIBBS RACING
2002
NASCAR WINSTON CUP CHAMPION
TONY STEWART
MBNA
PONTIAC

5 HIGHS AND LOWS

An excited Tony Stewart stood inside the Homestead-Miami Speedway, beaming as many of his competitors came up to him on the afternoon of November 17, 2002. The Ford 400 had just ended. Although Stewart did not win the race, he had driven well enough in this, the last race of the Winston Cup series, to clinch the top spot in the 2002 standings.

As the victorious Stewart tried to take it all in, several other drivers came up to him and congratulated him. That respect blew him away.

Stewart raises his championship trophy after capturing the 2002 Winston Cup title.

"To have your peers come out and congratulate you like that—I don't care what check (series sponsor) Winston writes," Stewart said. "I don't care how many trophies they give me, the satisfaction of seeing those guys out there is more than money can buy."[1]

A ROUGH YEAR

Once he came to grips with what he had just accomplished, Stewart was almost as relieved as he was thrilled. Yes, he had won a title in the elite NASCAR series. Yes, he had staked his claim as one of the top stock car drivers in the world. But he had also experienced a long, difficult 2002 season.

Stewart started the season with a last-place finish in the opening race and ended it by barely placing in the top twenty in the last race. In between, he hit a photographer, was accused of assaulting a fan, and drove himself and his racing team nuts.

"To be able to rebound the way we did, I still have a hard time believing we accomplished what we did this year," Stewart said. "I practically destroyed this team at midseason single-handedly."[2]

As he accepted the Winston Cup trophy and prepared for an off-season as the reigning NASCAR champion, the thirty-one-year-old Stewart knew he had to change. He had learned so much about himself and how to treat others from his experiences during the previous nine months.

Stewart had ended the 2001 Winston Cup season on a roll. He won in Bristol (Virginia) on August 25, placed in the top ten in eleven of the last thirteen races, and finished second overall in the standings. Many publications and racing experts picked him to win his first Cup in 2002.

Stewart did not get the 2002 season off to a good start, however. He began the Daytona 500 in sixth on February 17 but ran just two laps before his engine expired. That knocked him out of the race; he finished last. He was very disappointed.

STEWART'S 2002 WINSTON CUP SEASON

Wins: Three

Top-five finishes: Fifteen

Races not completed: Six

Place: First

"It was the motor. I just don't know what happened," Stewart said. The motor "laid down a little bit on the start, and then it just let go. I'm just glad I was able to get down out of the way when it happened and we didn't collect anyone or cause a problem."[3]

Three top-five finishes, including a win March 10 at Atlanta Motor Speedway, got Stewart into contention in the Winston Cup series. But accidents on March 17 at Darlington Raceway in South

Carolina and April 21 at Talladega Motor Speedway in Alabama, followed by a poor showing April 28 at California Speedway, sunk him to tenth in the standings.

Stewart was badly injured in the Darlington accident. While racing in the Carolina Dodge Dealers 400, he was bumped by the lap car and careened into the path of Jimmy Spencer's car. That car struck Stewart's passenger door. Stewart had to be taken to a hospital in a helicopter to be treated for back pain, numbness, and tingling in his left foot.

Fortunately, an MRI revealed that no permanent damage had been done, and Stewart returned to race the next week. Yet he still struggled to get rolling.

"It seems like every time we make one step forward in the points and get some momentum going, something dumb happens," said Greg Zipadelli, Stewart's crew chief.[4]

Struggles on the racetrack soon became the least of Stewart's problems, however.

LETTING HIS ANGER GET THE BETTER OF HIM

Stewart soon climbed back into the Winston Cup race. Three top-seven finishes in the previous five races put him in seventh place in the standings—in time for the Brickyard 400. That race, in his favorite venue, was scheduled for August 4 at Indianapolis Motor Speedway.

GREG ZIPADELLI FILE

Born: April 21, 1967

From: Berlin, Connecticut

Lives: Huntersville, North Carolina

Notes: Crew chief for Tony Stewart on NASCAR Winston Cup series, 1999 to present; chassis specialist for driver Jeff Burton on NASCAR Winston Cup series, 1998; crew chief for drivers on NASCAR Busch North series with owner Mike Greci, 1994 to 1997; crew chief for driver Mike McLaughlin on NASCAR Busch North series, 1990 to 1993

Stewart dominated some of the Brickyard, leading for forty-three laps of a race he wanted to win more than any other. Since he was a boy growing up in Indiana, he had yearned to win at Indianapolis Motor Speedway. He had never done so. Yet he was in solid position with only ten laps to go. He was holding on to third place.

Then disaster struck. For some reason, Stewart was unable to keep up, and he fell back into the pack. He finished twelfth, well behind the winner.

After the race, as media members descended upon Stewart to ask him what had happened, a frustrated Stewart snapped, reached out, and slapped a photographer.

Stewart talks with his crew chief, Greg Zipadelli, after practice.

NASCAR executives were furious. They fined Stewart $10,000 and forced him to get counseling to help manage his anger. They also placed him on "zero tolerance" probation, meaning any similar incident would get Stewart suspended from the Winston Cup series.

The Home Depot, Stewart's sponsor, fined him $50,000. Many fans, media, and NASCAR insiders ripped Stewart. For the first time in his life, the popular driver was a public enemy.

"If Stewart wants to refuse interviews, hide from prying lenses, that's his prerogative," wrote a columnist. "But violence? Lashing out physically at people who are credentialed to stand in the paddock area so they can do their jobs? It is unacceptable.

"NASCAR is telling its resident *enfant terrible* to act like a grown-up. It shouldn't be all that difficult."[5]

Later in August, Stewart was accused by a fan of assaulting her at Bristol (Tennessee) Motor Speedway. The charges were eventually dropped, but Stewart's reputation was even further damaged.

THE 2002 BRICKYARD 400

Location: **Indianapolis Motor Speedway in Indianapolis, Indiana**

Winner: **Bill Elliott**

Tony Stewart's place: **Twelfth**

BOUNCING BACK

Stewart was depressed. But just when it seemed like he could fold, he responded. The next week in Watkins Glen, he led for thirty-four of ninety laps and won the Sirius Satellite Radio at the Glen. Many experts were not surprised.

"Maybe it's not remarkable at all" that Stewart won in Watkins Glen, a magazine writer said. "Maybe Tony Stewart thrives on the constant swirl of agitations he seems to create for himself."[6]

Actually, Stewart said, he was still bothered by the incident with the photographer while racing in Watkins Glen. He had learned a lesson from his actions but was not over the shame they caused. "I realize he was just doing his job," Stewart said of the photographer. "It's something I'm not proud of, but it's over, I've paid the price, and I just want it to go away.

"It doesn't lift anything off my shoulders. I still did what I did last week, and I'm still ashamed of it."[7]

If Stewart was not over the incident with the photographer mentally, it did not affect him on the racetrack. The victory in Watkins Glen launched a great close to the season for him. Stewart placed in the top ten in ten of the next fourteen races.

While other contenders collapsed, he was a steady driver. He placed second August 18 at Michigan International Speedway and again October 6 at Talladega. That race vaulted Stewart into the Winston Cup lead for the first time in his career.

"There's no way I ever could have dreamed we'd be where we are today," Stewart said after the race in Talladega. "It just shows that you can't give up."[8]

Stewart still had a 72-point advantage after Talladega, but six races remained on the 2002 schedule. He held onto the lead. When he ran eighth at Phoenix International Raceway November 10, he put a lot of distance between himself and competitors. He carried an 89-point lead into the season's final race

An eighteenth-place finish in Miami gave Tony Stewart his first Winston Cup title in 2002.

the following week in Miami. All he needed to do was finish in the middle of the pack.

Late in the race, Stewart was in good position. But with thirty-three laps to go, John Andretti blew an engine just in front of him, spraying oil all over Turn 3. Stewart remained calm and moved down the track to safely cruise past Andretti. A little while later, he finished the race in eighteenth place and clinched his first Winston Cup title.

STILL PAYING FOR HIS BEHAVIOR

Stewart won the Cup despite failing to complete six races and having to deal with all of the controversy that his short temper had created. Afterward, he accepted little credit for the championship. He was quick to credit his crew. He especially thanked crew chief Greg Zipadelli, buying Zipadelli a cherry red Corvette to honor him.

"Zippy was the glue that held everybody together," Stewart said. "Zippy was the friend that got me back on track and got my mind-set right to do what we did the rest of the year."[9]

The Winston Cup title was a bittersweet triumph for Stewart. Despite his consistent, impressive driving, he earned little praise from the media and NASCAR insiders. Many people were still caught up by his surly behavior and outbursts during the season.

"Nobody questions his talent or intensity, but that doesn't change their opinion that he is immature and a poor loser with anger-management issues," a magazine writer said.[10]

In addition to backlash from outsiders, Stewart also had to endure criticism and complaints from his own team. Gibbs racing officials were pleased with his performance but

THE 2002 PEPSI 400

Location: Michigan International Speedway in Brooklyn, Michigan

Winner: Dale Jarrett

Tony Stewart's place: Second

furious about his behavior. And his crew was drained by his rants, long work hours, and childish behavior at the racetrack. Fortunately, they knew Stewart acted that way because he wanted to win so badly.

THE 2002 EA SPORTS 500

Location: Talladega Superspeedway

Winner: Dale Earnhardt Jr.

Tony Stewart's place: Second

"It could have been the end. Folks were mad," said Jimmy Makar, team manager for Joe Gibbs Racing. "In the end, I don't think anyone gave up on him, and that's why he's still here."[11]

Other people defended Stewart and gave him a lot of credit for clinching the title. Gibbs offered an excuse, noting that Stewart was still unaccustomed to being in the Winston Cup spotlight.

"Tony is a product of racing different cars in different series for different fans on consecutive nights," Gibbs said. "It's always been, 'I'll say whatever I want, get out of here, and be gone.' There's more to it in Winston Cup."[12]

In the three months between his blow-up in Indianapolis and his final race of the season in Miami, Stewart had changed considerably, Gibbs said.

And the change was for the better. "There's been a dramatic improvement since Indy in the way Tony has approached things, his self-control," Gibbs said. "I think he's had some times when he'd still get upset, but they seem to be fewer. I think we're making progress there.

"One good thing about Tony is that he's always come right back and said, 'Hey, it's my fault.' I think he's done a terrific job. We've had a lot of things happen to the car this year, and he doesn't seem to get nearly as uptight and rattled by it."[13]

Gibbs was not the only person to support Stewart during the rough 2002 season. Before a Winston Cup race at Richmond International Raceway, Dale Jarrett stood up in front of Stewart and several other drivers at a driver's meeting and said out loud:

"I've talked to a lot of these guys in this room, Tony, and you're a big reason all these fans are filling the stands every week. You've got all our support, and we'll do everything we can to help keep you in this sport. Keep your head up."[14]

Other drivers agreed with Jarrett's sentiments.

"I think, single-handedly, (Stewart) has moved this sport up a notch, maybe two," Darrell Waltrip said.[15]

Stewart earned the 2002 title for his driving prowess. He deserved it, friends said, because of how much he matured over the course of a trying season.

"He understands that he needs to take responsibility for the things he has done," Zipadelli said. "He knows there's a right way and a wrong way of expressing himself. Tony has way more good qualities than bad, but because of who he is, sometimes he has to work twice as hard because little things get turned into big ones."[16]

"As much stuff as we went through, I'm hoping—praying—that I've got the worst of it behind me," Stewart said.[17]

There was only one way to find out—start the 2003 season.

HOME DEPOT
USA
1978
FORTSON
FOSTER
THE HOME DEPOT
Mahr

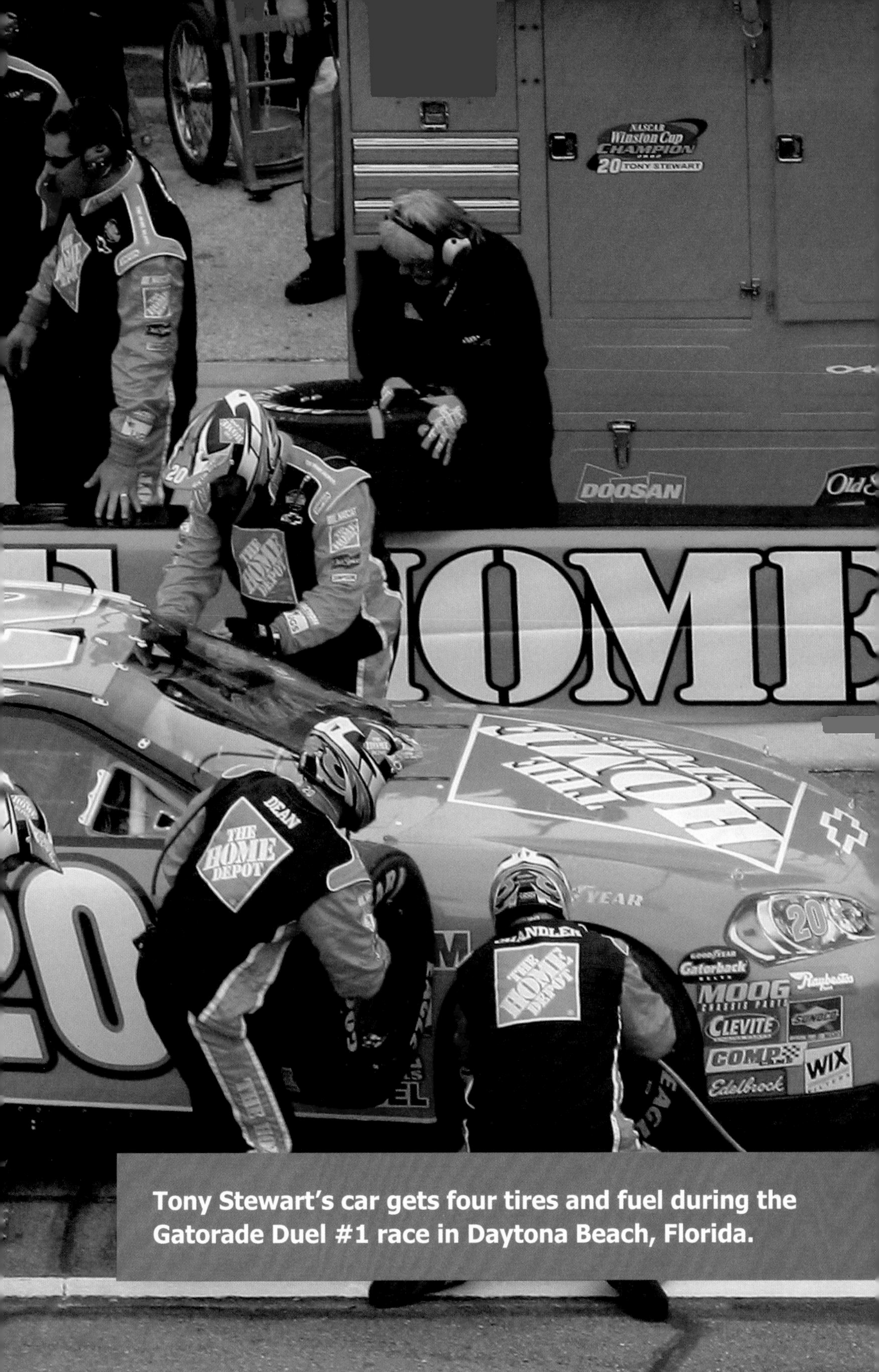

Tony Stewart's car gets four tires and fuel during the Gatorade Duel #1 race in Daytona Beach, Florida.

6 A CONTROVERSIAL STAR

Nextel Cup driver Carl Edwards says Tony Stewart is a jerk.

Actually, Stewart is a great guy who has a really good heart, according to Nextel driver Dale Earnhardt, Jr.

The real Tony Stewart probably lies somewhere in between. Because of his temperamental, aggressive personality, people who know him rarely sit in the middle when it comes to their feelings about one of NASCAR's greatest drivers.

Many fans, racing experts, drivers, and other racing professionals agree with Edwards. Others side with

Earnhardt, defending Stewart for being concerned about others and caring so much about his chosen profession.

Stewart is aware of how the public perceives him. He cares deeply about that. He also knows that he is responsible for creating such different views of his image.

He often starts collisions and confrontations with other drivers during races. He once angrily pushed a news photographer and knocked a tape recorder out of a reporter's hand. He also says whatever is on his mind—without thinking of the consequences.

CARL EDWARDS FILE

Born: August 15, 1979

Team: Roush Racing

Sponsor: Office Depot

Manufacturer: Ford

Car: No. 99

Notes: Won four Nextel Cup races in 2005 season, his first full year on the circuit

BEING HIMSELF

Stewart is a controversial yet popular athlete. The NBA has Allen Iverson. The NFL has Terrell Owens. Major League Baseball has Barry Bonds. And NASCAR has Tony Stewart.

Just like those other famous pro athletes, Stewart is a lot deeper than any news report or quote could possibly describe in detail.

"I'm not just the person that everybody reads about in the media," Stewart said. "I know I've caused a lot of my own headaches. I've made my bed, and I'm sleeping in it."[1]

Some of Stewart's actions have prevented him from being as beloved as many of his competitors. His actions have also drawn scorn, even though he is a successful driver who signs numerous autographs and volunteers to do a lot of charitable work.

"Tony Stewart will never be NASCAR's king," wrote a newspaper columnist. "He's a jerk."[2]

"How can a person make it this far in life and be that much of a jerk?" Carl Edwards wondered.[3]

The answer: While he may be a jerk sometimes, he is a very complex person.

Stewart is not afraid to stand up and do what he thinks he should do—or, in some cases, what he wants to do. That is true even if he knows his actions will cause controversy and offend some people.

For example, early in his career he competed in two major races on the same day, running in both the Coca-Cola 600 in Charlotte and the Indianapolis 500. He competed in Indianapolis, then flew to Charlotte for the nightcap. He did so even though, as he later admitted, all that racing and flying drained him and forced him to compete in the second race at far from his best level.

Stewart was slammed by the media and some competitors for participating in both races. He did so because he still enjoyed Indy racing and needed to race in Charlotte to keep up in the Winston Cup standings, he said.

He does not regret that choice, even if other people think he made a poor one. In fact, he has said he would continue to race in the Indy 500 every year—if he did not think it was unfair to his NASCAR team to do so.

Stewart also says what he thinks. Unlike many modern athletes who say what the public wants to hear or do not say much at all, Stewart is open and honest.

"Stewart's mouth doesn't have a brake," one writer said. "He is incapable of being anything but candid."[4]

Take an incident in December 2006, for example. Stewart sampled a larger, safer NASCAR racecar in New York. Afterward, he called the car a "flying brick" and ripped it for having an ugly design and forcing race teams to adjust too much to it.

"I think it could become the biggest disaster NASCAR has faced in a long time," he said. "When you run them on ovals 36 weeks of the year, I don't think they're going to look too good."[5]

Stewart speaks his mind because he thinks it is the right thing to do. Being a boring interview subject and not saying what he believes in "is 100 percent totally unfair to the race fans," he said. "I think it's cheating them out of knowing who we are."[6]

Many drivers support Stewart for expressing his opinions so freely. They admire him for doing so, because some of them are not able to do the same.

"Tony is good for the sport," Kenny Wallace said. "This sport is full of characters, and you don't want them all to be the same. He's refreshing, because he says what's on his mind."[7]

"I've got a tremendous amount of respect for Tony because he has never once tried to hide who he is," Jimmy Spencer said. "Sit back and think about all the pressures in this sport—sponsors, owners, crews, all these different people with all different opinions. Yet you've got to make them all happy. It's a tough thing to do and still be yourself."[8]

DID YOU KNOW?

The new NASCAR car's shape is more boxy, with the drivers' seats moved four inches (ten centimeters) closer to the center. The enhancements should make the cars safer, NASCAR officials said. The Car of Tomorrow debuted in the 2007 Nextel Cup season.

BRIAN VICKERS FILE

Born: October 24, 1983

Team: Team Red Bull

Sponsor: Red Bull

Manufacturer: Toyota

Car: No. 83

Notes: Finished in top ten four times in 2004 season, his first full-time year on Nextel Cup series

GETTING PHYSICAL

Stewart sometimes acts the way he wants, too. He has had many blow-ups during and after races, when he goes after other drivers, the media, and even NASCAR officials.

He once walked up to a car and punched a competitor who had just knocked him out of a race. After a 2004 race he ran into a garage belonging to the team for Brian Vickers, yelled at Vickers, and hit the driver with his palm.

Stewart has even mixed it up with drivers who respect and admire him. On the second lap of a 2000 race in Watkins Glen, Jeff Gordon tried to pass him. Stewart promptly crowded Gordon, sending his No. 24 car into the guardrail. The car was badly damaged, and Gordon's racing suffered because of it.

After the race, Gordon came up next to Stewart and yelled, "Next time you get alongside me, I'll slam you into the wall first chance I get."

"Come over here, and we'll talk about it," Stewart replied.[9] The two drivers had to be separated.

During the 2004 Winston Cup season, Stewart inspired a lot of nasty comments from opponents because of his aggressive driving.

"Jamie McMurray called Stewart 'an idiot' and highly respected veteran Rusty Wallace has said he wanted to 'whip his rear end,'" a magazine reported. "After Kasey Kahne was involved in a wreck with Stewart at Chicagoland Speedway on July 11, Kahne's car owner, Ray Evernham, told reporters that he'd 'like to have 10 minutes with Tony Stewart and handle [him] myself.'"[10]

In his career, Stewart has earned more than $100,000 in fines and been placed on probation four times by NASCAR officials for his behavior.

"He goes around and does some childish stuff," said driver Richard Petty, a former Winston Cup champion. "He does it without thinking. I don't think he's grown up as far as really understanding how the public looks at him."[11]

"There's a fine line between being in control and out of control, and Tony occasionally crosses it," one Nextel Cup driver said. "I wouldn't say he's a time bomb, but he's something close."[12]

A DIFFERENT MAN ON AND OFF THE TRACK

The Tony Stewart who races cars is different from the real Tony Stewart, friends and other supporters say. He often regrets when he makes a mistake or harms somebody and has tried to address his temper so that he does not make those same mistakes again. A little while after he hit the news photographer in 2002, for example, he invited the man to dinner in order to apologize to him.

"You don't always see it at the track, but Tony has a really good heart," Earnhardt, Jr. said. "At the track he's a competitor, just like I am, just like my dad (Dale Earnhardt, Sr.) was. He really, really loves the sport."[13]

Stewart, his friends say, is "a man with two distinct personalities. There's Tempestuous Tony, the driver blessed with electric talent but saddled with a hot temper. And there's Regular Dude Tony, the down-to-earth, highly intelligent guy from a working-class neighborhood."[14]

As a professional athlete, Stewart thinks he should be treated and viewed no differently than other pro athletes. Those athletes often get into skirmishes

RICHARD PETTY FILE

Born: July 2, 1937

Notes: Inducted into the International Motorsports Hall of Fame; won 200 Winston Cup races in career; and captured seven Winston Cup series championships

Stewart signs autographs for fans at Elko Speedway in Minnesota.

during games, with bench-clearing brawls in baseball and small fights after plays in football. Like Stewart, they sometimes let their emotions get the best of them and then react.

Yet Stewart does not think he is viewed by many people with the same respect and understanding as those pro athletes are. "You watch baseball, basketball, football, and hockey, and there's not a game that somebody doesn't throw a punch," Stewart said. "I didn't know having an argument with a guy was a crime. . . . We all have our bad days. But I have a bad day and I'm angry, everybody's ready to jump all over it.

"What I have a problem with is when these articles come out, it's 'Tony the Terrible' or 'Tony's Temper.' But that's not how I am away from the track. It was just part of the moment, and there's nothing wrong with that."[15]

Stewart in fact has been complimented by other drivers for his temperament. He is strong enough to withstand the insults and aggression that his personality and actions draw, they say. "He might get in somebody's face when he feels like he's been wronged, but he doesn't care when you get in his face for the same thing," Nextel Cup driver Kyle Petty said. "He can dish it out, but he can take it."[16]

Stewart does not get into trouble

DALE EARNHARDT, JR. FILE

Born: October 10, 1974

Team: Dale Earnhardt Inc.

Sponsor: Budweiser

Manufacturer: Chevrolet

Car: No. 8

Notes: Had seventeen career Nextel Cup wins, including two at Daytona International Speedway, through 2007 season

KYLE PETTY FILE

Born:
June 2, 1960

Team:
Petty Enterprises

Sponsors: Several

Manufacturer:
Dodge

Car: No. 45

Notes:
Had eight Nextel Cup victories through 2005 season, his twenty-fifth season racing full time on the circuit

away from the track either. As fired up as he is at races, he is usually calm and harmless when he is on his own or with family and friends.

"That attitude in our sport is nothing like it is in other sports, where the guys get themselves in trouble away from the racetrack," said former driver Darrell Waltrip, now a race analyst for FOX Sports. "Tony might shove a reporter out of his way or bump into a fan in the garage area, but he doesn't take that out on the streets."[17]

STRUGGLING IN THE SPOTLIGHT

Part of Stewart's problem is that he may find it difficult to handle being a celebrity. When he first burst onto the NASCAR Winston Cup scene with a stellar rookie season in 1999, he was overwhelmed. Since then he has slowly adjusted to all of the attention he has received. Yet he is still not completely accustomed to it.

"A great deal of his frustration was that he couldn't escape," said Joan Mabe, a neighbor of the Stewart family when Tony was growing up. "Tony was a hometown kid who became extremely popular in a short period of time. He couldn't cope with that."[18]

Stewart is getting better at coping, though, according to friends and NASCAR insiders. As long as he keeps under control, many people who know him are content with the way he is.

"Should he change his personality to represent the sport any different?" Kyle Petty wondered. "No. I don't think Tony should change."[19]

The 2007 season brought more of the same antics. In April, NASCAR levied a $10,000 fine on Stewart and placed him on probation for the rest of the year because Stewart failed to attend a media conference following his second-place finish in Phoenix.

In July, NASCAR fined Stewart $25,000 after he used a profanity during a postrace television interview. Earlier in the season, an ESPN analyst had said that Stewart wasn't a good role model.

"I don't want anybody from ESPN talking about how irresponsible I am, even though it's legal to do everything I did," he said. "Heaven forbid you actually have fun in life."[20]

7 A GROWING MATURITY

After winning the Winston Cup in 2002, Tony Stewart was more relieved than excited. He spent the off-season celebrating his triumph—and trying to address his behavior to avoid another difficult emotional season like 2002.

By the time the 2003 season started in February, it was obvious that he had matured and calmed down a bit. Winning the Cup helped him accomplish that, as did moving back home to Indiana.

That is not to say Stewart became a passive, relaxed driver. He still maintained the same aggressive, win-at-all-costs approach to races that he had since he was seven. By 2003, he just became easier to deal with for his crew, media members, and fans.

"He is the same person, but he acts differently," said Mike Helton, NASCAR's president. "The character of this Tony existed before; it's just gotten more prominent. It's fair to say he has been a handful at times, but it didn't last long. He had moments, just like in all sports. What everybody sees today is the person who was hidden by the issues a few years ago."[1]

GROWING AS A PERSON

Stewart's transformation began shortly after he clinched the Winston Cup title at the final 2002 race, held at Homestead-Miami International Raceway on November 17. He soon embarked on a whirlwind tour to honor his championship. He visited the White House and rang the opening bell at the New York Stock Exchange, among other trips.

That recognition made him feel much better about himself. It also got rid of some of the angst he had carried around. He had always thought he needed to win a title to prove himself as a driver. Now he had.

"If people could have lived the last three weeks of the season with us (in 2002), they would have seen how much pressure he put on himself to win that championship," said Eddie Jarvis, Stewart's friend and personal manager. "He wanted it for his team more than for himself for what he did to that team."[2]

"The biggest reason (for my newfound maturity) is we're not sitting here answering the question, 'Can we win a championship?'" Stewart said. "That's a pretty big question in our series. . . . It seems like once we won the championship last year, it was like I dumped a 3,000-pound weight off my back."[3]

Another catalyst to launching the new Stewart was a meeting he had with members of his crew, Joe Gibbs racing officials, and his sponsors after the tumultuous 2002 season. None of them spared Stewart. They came after him, telling him exactly how they felt.

Stewart was uncomfortable, but he sat through the meeting and listened intently. As a result, he and his crew were able to make compromises and meet each other's needs more often in 2003.

"The thing that has changed is he has become a leader," said J.D. Gibbs, president of Joe Gibbs Racing.

TONY STEWART'S 2003 WINSTON CUP SEASON

Wins: Two

Top-five finishes: Twelve

Races not completed: Five

Place: Seventh

President George Bush holds up a driver's suit given to him by Tony Stewart, right. At left is race team owner Joe Gibbs.

"He has matured, gotten older, stepped up. The issues were always a few hours before or a few hours after [the races]. We stepped back and said, 'Is this who he is?' and 'Are we going to have to deal with this forever?'

"The real breakout was when the (crew) sat down with Tony and said what they thought. They did a great job, they didn't hold back. They told him why it wasn't working and laid it out as a personal thing. They said how hard he was on them.

"They needed him to work with them as well. When he realized what he was putting them through, that was a big part of his maturing process."[4]

HOME SWEET HOME

Stewart also benefited from moving back home to Indiana. He purchased the house in which he grew up. His mother had sold the house a few years earlier, but it was soon back on the market. Stewart bought it and moved back in on his own.

That helped him recharge when he was not racing. Living at home in southern Indiana was a better lifestyle for Stewart than living near his team and other NASCAR folks in Charlotte, North Carolina. In Charlotte, Stewart lived just fifteen minutes from his garage and was always thinking about his job.

"I decided, I'm just going to up and go home," Stewart said. "To be able to maintain a competitive edge, you have to be able to turn it off, reset yourself, and then turn it back on again. . . . It's hard to maintain that intensity all year doing it seven days a week."[5]

The Indiana home is "a place where he can find peace and contentment without a lot of hype, without a lot of pressure from people wanting something from him," said Pam Boas, Stewart's mother. "Those people in Columbus (Indiana) don't want anything from him. They just want him to be home and be happy."[6]

HANDLING A ROCKY ROAD

The newfound mellowness he developed helped Stewart endure inconsistent 2003 and 2004 seasons. His team switched from a Pontiac to a Chevrolet racecar and had to make several adjustments to prepare for 2003. Partly because of that, Stewart got off to another slow start that year.

After placing fortieth in a May 25 race in Charlotte, he sank to twentieth in the Cup standings. During seven races between March 23 and May 25, he wrecked twice, blew two engines, and finished fortieth or worse three times. During another ten-race stretch, he led for only three laps combined and failed to finish a race four times.

"I think that all of you guys expected me to flip out, the way things have gone," Stewart joked to several media members in early June. However, Stewart did not lose his cool. The slow start was not anyone's fault, he said. "It's just circumstances out there. It happens to everybody."[7]

"He's been doing good," Zipadelli said of Stewart. "He's frustrated, but he's handled it better than he has in the past. I think a lot of that is probably looking at some of the things he's done in the past, and if he reacted the same way it'd be real easy to run everybody down and kill the motivation of the team and the guys. He's working hard not to do that."[8]

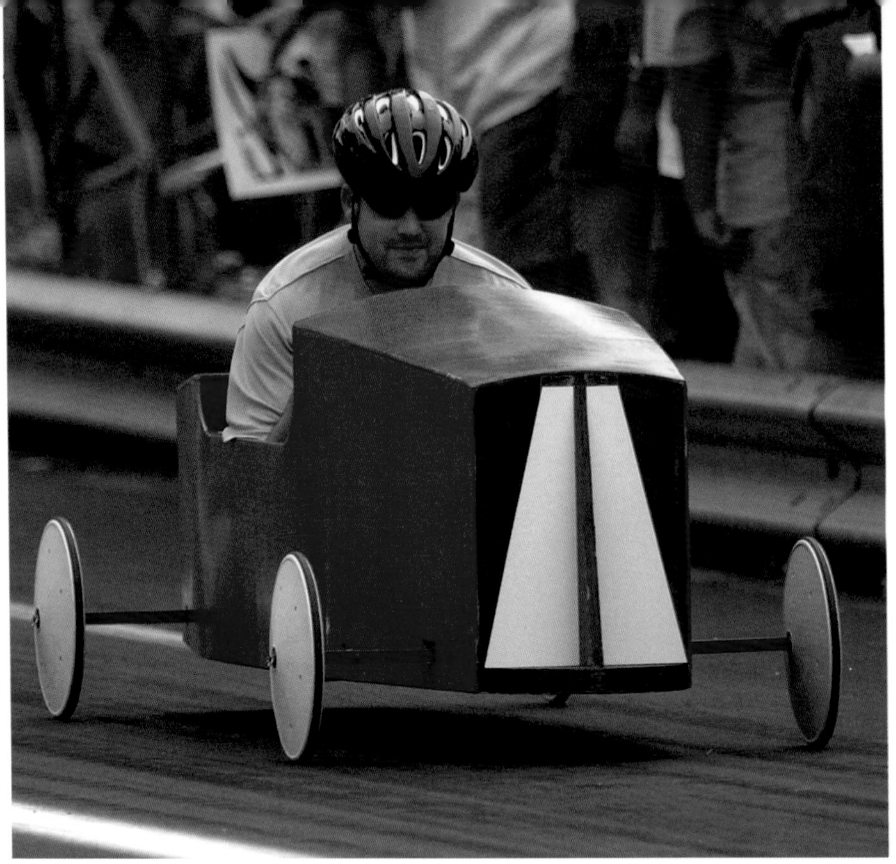

Stewart drives a vehicle at the 2003 All-American Soap Box Derby.

A calmer Stewart also allowed everyone on his team to enjoy themselves more at the track. "As a race team this year, we've had more fun," Stewart said. "It's something we had started to lose in the past. As much as we all love this sport, we were losing the passion behind why we love it so much. We needed to get that back, and luckily, winning the championship did that for us."[9]

Winning a championship did not guarantee more success, though. Stewart had to struggle to compete with other top drivers on the Winston Cup circuit in 2003 and 2004.

He won a career-low two races in 2003, but he saved that season with a strong finish. He won June 8 at Pocono Raceway in Pennsylvania and again on October 11 at Lowe's Motor Speedway in Charlotte. The latter race came in the middle of a stretch when he placed at least fourth in six straight races. That helped him finish seventh overall.

Stewart failed to capitalize on that strong finish, though. He again won only two races in 2004. That season was doomed from the start, when he crashed during an exhibition race. He failed to finish in the top ten in more than three consecutive races at any

STEWART CATCHES FIRE IN 2003

September 21 at Dover (Delaware) International Speedway: **Third**

September 28 at Talladega (Alabama) Superspeedway: **Third**

October 5 at Kansas Speedway (Kansas City): **Fourth**

October 11 at Lowe's Motor Speedway (Charlotte): **First**

October 19 at Martinsville (Virginia) Speedway: **Third**

October 26–27 at Atlanta Motor Speedway: **Second**

point in the season, and he had a career-low ten top-five finishes.

Stewart twice climbed as high as second in the standings and qualified for the first annual Chase for the Nextel Cup, a new series NASCAR instituted to determine a champion during the last ten races. He could not pull through, however. He finished sixth in the Chase.

That did not bother Stewart. Despite his struggles in 2003 and 2004, he still finished those seasons in the top ten. That gave him six straight top-ten finishes to start his career on the Winston Cup circuit. He was confident heading into the 2005 season—and relaxed.

"He doesn't seem to get nearly as uptight and rattled," Gibbs said. "He's much more relaxed about what's happening around him."[10]

"Once he won (the first title), he had a lot of responsibilities," Boas said. "He had to think about, 'What am I doing? What am I saying.'

"It was time to grow up."[11]

And grow up Stewart did.

STEWART'S WINSTON CUP FINISHES IN HIS FIRST SIX SEASONS (1999–2004)

1999: Fourth

2000: Sixth

2001: Second

2002: First

2003: Seventh

2004: Sixth

PROVING HIMSELF A CHAMPION

For most of his life, Tony Stewart dreamed of winning a race at Indianapolis Motor Speedway. When he finally did, capturing the Allstate 400 on August 7, 2005, he was overjoyed.

As he crossed the finish line and the checkered flag waved, he called out to his team over his radio, "You guys have helped me win my lifelong dream today."[1]

Many weekends in 2005 were like the weekend of August 7 for Stewart. Winning at Indianapolis was part of a dream season.

Stewart dominated the Winston Cup series in 2005, posting one of the best seasons in NASCAR history. He won consecutive races on two occasions, captured five races overall, and placed in the top ten in nineteen of the season's final twenty-two races. He also had an amazing two-month stretch in the summer to key the season.

Stewart vaulted into third place by winning at Daytona International Speedway on July 2, took over the top spot after his emotional victory at the Indianapolis Motor Speedway, and cruised to a championship by driving solid races in the season-ending Chase for the Nextel Cup.

"The wins just helped the morale of the team," Stewart said, "and our performance just carried it that much further."[2]

GETTING BACK ON TRACK

The roots of Stewart's great 2005 season can be traced to the end of 2004. Stewart had a disappointing finish to the 2004 season. He fell from championship contention and fourth place at mid-season to sixth place at the end, failing to finish higher than sixth in any of the season's last fourteen races.

After the season, Stewart solved some problems with his overworked, underappreciated crew. They met again and hashed out some differences. Then he committed to his bosses with Joe Gibbs Racing, signing a new contract, and all parties set out to have a smoother 2005.

They did. Stewart began the season by winning an all-star race at Daytona February 17. After a decent start to the official Nextel Cup season, he caught fire at the beginning of the summer. It began with a second-place finish at Michigan International Speedway on June 20. Then came his first two-race winning streak—at California's Infineon Raceway June 26 and Daytona International Speedway July 2.

Stewart won again at New Hampshire International Speedway on July 17. After a seventh-place finish July 24 at Pocono Raceway, he posted his second two-race winning streak of the season. He won at Indianapolis and again at Watkins Glen International.

Those performances gave Stewart five victories in

STEWART'S HOT STREAK IN 2005

June 26:
Won at Infineon Raceway (Sonoma, California)

July 2:
Won at Daytona International Speedway (Florida)

July 10:
Fifth at Chicagoland Speedway (Joliet, Illinois)

July 17:
Won at New Hampshire International Speedway

July 24:
Seventh at Pocono Raceway (Pennsylvania)

August 7:
Won at Indianapolis Motor Speedway

August 14:
Won at Watkins Glen International (New York)

seven races. It was one of the best runs in NASCAR history. The incredible thing about that hot streak was that Stewart won on four different types of tracks: road courses, a superspeedway, a short track, and a long, flat track.

"What Stewart is doing is extraordinary," said Donald Davison, the historian for Indianapolis Motor Speedway. "To win at Indy one week and on a road course the next is pretty amazing."[3]

Stewart led the series standings heading into the Chase for the Nextel Cup. That ten-race conclusion to the season began September 18 at New Hampshire. Stewart placed second. After he struggled at Dover International Speedway, he finished second again in the Chase's third race, this time at Talladega Superspeedway.

Stewart placed second at Martinsville Speedway on October 23. He put himself in solid position to take the Cup by placing sixth at Texas Motor Speedway on November 6 and fourth at Phoenix International Raceway on November 6.

Those performances gave him a huge lead heading into the season's final race at Homestead-Miami Speedway. Even placing fifteenth in that race, the Ford 400 on November 20, did not make Stewart sweat. He clinched the Cup easily. He beat second-place finishers Greg Biffle and Carl Edwards by thirty-five points.

Stewart was thrilled to capture another title in NASCAR's top series. He was especially excited because the 2005 championship came much easier for him and his crew than the 2002 title had.

"I'm just so happy we could get this championship the right way with [everything] I put this team through in 2002," he said. "It's nice to finally do one right."[4]

A NEW ATTITUDE

Stewart attributed his incredible season to his new outlook on life. After the meeting with his crew, he learned to take it easier on them and focus on enjoying racing. That helped everyone calm down and perform better on race day.

"Even when we weren't running good, we were having fun," Stewart said. "We got back to why we started racing in the first place and that's because we love being a part of race teams, and we love racing and we love competing. That attitude carried us through the slow times, and when the good times happened, it just made it that much better for us."[5]

STEWART'S 2005 WINSTON CUP SEASON

Wins: Five

Top-five finishes: Seventeen

Races not completed: Zero

Place: First

Stewart (20) battles Jeff Gordon (24), Matt Kenseth (17), and Scott Riggs (10).

DEWALT
USG
SHEETROCK
TAURUS
MOOG
CLEVITE
WIX
E DEPOT
884
Valvoline
MONTE CARLO
24
DUPONT
24
PEPSI
GMAC

Stewart's crew and bosses at Joe Gibbs Racing credited him for establishing that positive attitude and setting the tone for the whole team.

"Clearly, he's having fun with what he's doing," said Greg Zipadelli, Stewart's crew chief. "There are still days and moments, but he's dealing with it a lot better.

"We've been through some ups and downs, but we won this championship because of him and his attitude. This is the most relaxed I've seen him in an entire season. It's also the first time I've seen him sit back and realize what he's capable of."[6]

Just like winning the first Cup championship in 2002 validated for Stewart that he was indeed a top driver, winning another title in 2005 validated something important for him. It proved that he had matured and could still be a champion without being so intense and unfriendly.

"A lot of things have changed," Stewart said. "I'm at a point where I'm comfortable enough with myself where I can look at the big picture and lead by the example (team owner) Joe Gibbs has given.

"To win at home in the Brickyard was the win of a lifetime for me, and to be able to finish it off with a championship—this is just perfect."[7]

Tony Stewart climbs the fence as fans cheer after he won the New England 300 in Loudon, New Hampshire.

HEVY
FFICIAL
& TRUCK
THE HOME DEPOT

GIVING BACK

Since he began racing in NASCAR and became a well-known celebrity, Tony Stewart has often used his fame to help other people. He has his own foundation to benefit many different types of people. He also volunteers to help other NASCAR drivers with their charity work and foundations.

That charitable side is just one of many facets of Stewart's personality. He is a complex person. He can be nasty and aggressive on the track but relaxed and helpful when he is not racing. He enjoys keeping to himself back home in Indiana, but he also has his own radio show that allows him to interact with fans and others all across the country.

SHARING HIS GOOD FORTUNE

Stewart started his foundation in 2003. His goal is to assist organizations that provide care to sick children and drivers who are injured in motorsports events. He also wants to help groups that take care of animals. His mother runs the foundation out of Indianapolis, and Stewart often volunteers his time and money to support it.

Stewart is also involved in Racing to Play, a charitable venture run by Joe Gibbs Racing, The Home Depot, which is Stewart's racing sponsor, and a nonprofit organization. Stewart and Zipadelli worked with others to build a NASCAR-themed playground in Michigan for children in at-risk communities in 2005. They were among the original volunteers for the Racing to Play program.

"This program brings together two of my deepest interests—racing and providing assistance

THE TONY STEWART FOUNDATION

Founded: 2003

Mission: Raise money to help groups that care for sick children and drivers injured in motorsports, and to assist groups that care for animals

to children in need," Stewart said. "In addition to building playgrounds, I hope that we can inspire these children to fulfill their dreams."[1]

Stewart has been honored for his charity work. In December 2004, for example, he was named NASCAR's Person of the Year. He was thrilled to get that award.

"This is a special award, because it's not about what you do on the racetrack, it's about what you do with your heart," Stewart said. "I know that the previous winners of this award were some very deserving people, and to join them means a tremendous amount to me."[2]

He was awarded $100,000 for the honor, with the money to be split between a charity of his choice and himself. Stewart instead donated all of the money to Victory Junction Gang Camp, a North Carolina camp for sick kids that is run by driver Kyle Petty and his wife.

That was one of many times that Stewart has assisted Victory Junction. He autographed towels in

WHAT IS RACING TO PLAY?

Racing to Play is a partnership involving the Joe Gibbs Racing team, a nonprofit organization, and The Home Depot that builds racing-themed playgrounds. More than 2,300 volunteers, including Tony Stewart, helped build ten Racing to Play playgrounds in 2005.

the winner's circle after each race he won in 2006. The towels were auctioned with the money the auctions raised going to support the camp. In 2004, he raised $240,000 for the camp by donating money for each lap that he completed in the Indianapolis 500 and Coca-Cola 600 races.

Stewart visits the petting zoo during an appearance at the Victory Junction Gang Camp in North Carolina. The camp serves special-needs children.

In part because of his generosity, Stewart was named Most Caring Athlete by *USA Weekend* and NASCAR's Good Guy in *The Sporting News'* annual list of "Good Guys."

Stewart also has volunteered to assist driver Ryan Newman with his foundation. Stewart attended a North Carolina fishing event in December 2006 with Newman, helping raise $40,000 for Newman's foundation. But Stewart's heart does not stop there. He likes to visit with people at work to cheer them up and show how much he appreciates what they do. For example, he visited a Texas General Motors assembly plant in December 2005 and another GM plant in Ohio the following year. He toured the facilities, sometimes stopping to help employees do their jobs. Meeting him thrilled many of the auto workers.

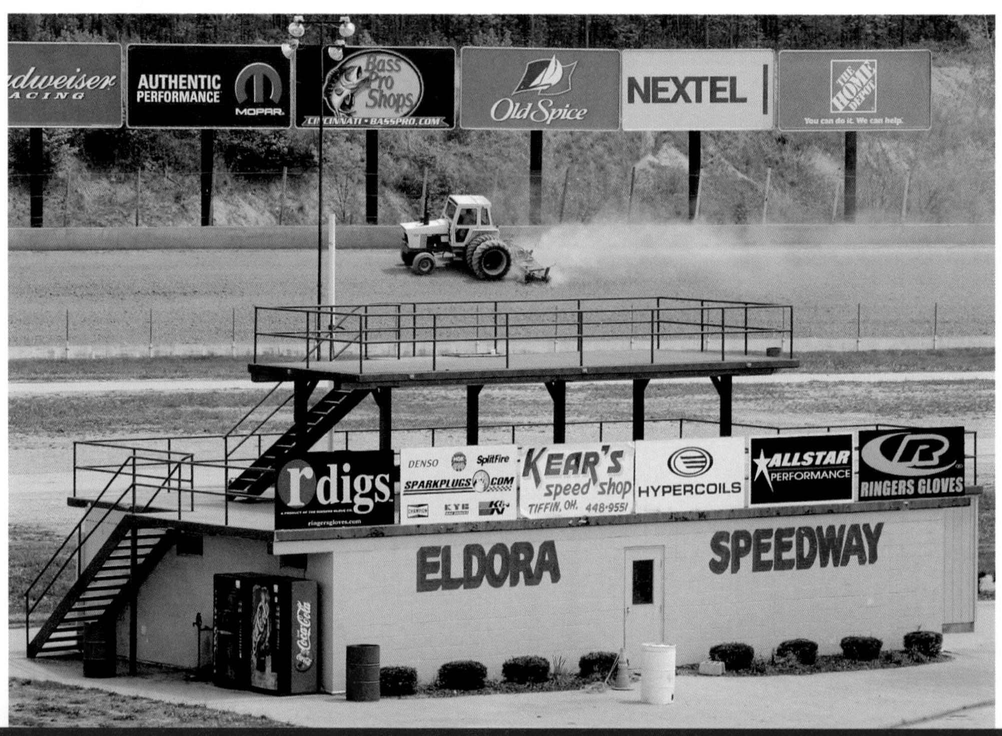

A tractor grades the dirt track at Eldora Speedway.

WHAT IS ELDORA SPEEDWAY?

Eldora Speedway is a small dirt racetrack in Rossburg, Ohio, owned and run by Tony Stewart. It holds many different types of races from March through October.

"He's gorgeous and an awesome driver," one woman said after meeting him at the Ohio plant. "You don't get this chance every day."[3]

A TRACK OF HIS OWN

Stewart, of course, spends a lot of his time competing on the NASCAR circuit. Yet he still finds time to indulge in other races. He likes to run midget and sprint cars, and sometimes shows up unannounced to race at small tracks.

Stewart even owns his own dirt track: Eldora Raceway, a small dirt track in western Ohio. Working on Eldora is sort of a hobby for him.

"To me, it's the perfect way to give back," Stewart said. "Grassroots racing has always been like a reset button for me. . . . It's pure, and it reminds you why you got started in this business in the first place.

"There are tracks that are losing (money)," Stewart added, noting that Eldora does not make him much money. "You do this not as an investment, but because you love it, because you love the sport."[4]

Stewart purchased Eldora in 2004 and has since installed a new clay surface, sewage system, lighting, and scoreboard. He often visits Eldora on weekends to watch big races, even if he has to fly straight from his own NASCAR races to see them.

"We've taken everything we've made with it and put it back into it," Stewart said. "Plus the sponsors that we get, we're putting all that money into the racetrack to make it better."[5]

Running the Eldora track keeps Stewart busy and also helps him with his career on the NASCAR circuit.

"It splits my attention so that I'm not always over-analyzing what's going on over here" on the Nextel Cup series, he said. "I don't get burned out as easy. At the end of the day, whatever happens, I can wash my hands of it and go back to my life."[6]

OFF THE TRACK

Stewart's life also includes eating a lot. For years he especially enjoyed greasy foods and junk foods. "Nobody loves to eat more than me," he said.[7]

He loves to eat so much that he has raced for much of his career in bad shape. He recently decided to live a healthier lifestyle, however. He began eating more fruits and vegetables and working out with a

WHAT IS VICTORY JUNCTION GANG CAMP?

Victory Junction Gang Camp in North Carolina was founded by Kyle and Pattie Petty in 2004 for children ages seven through fifteen who have chronic medical conditions or serious illnesses.

personal trainer. As a result, he dropped twenty pounds (nine kilograms) in 2006 and got down to 180 pounds (82 kg). He plans to continue his new lifestyle in order to stay in good shape.

Somehow Stewart still finds free time to get involved with the media. He has called a NASCAR Grand National race on television and recently debuted a new radio show. It's a show about NASCAR, Tony Stewart Live, which he co-hosts every Tuesday night on Sirius Satellite Radio. The show started for good in January 2007, after a trial in November 2006.

"It's just something fun to do on the side," he said. "It's just nice to kind of get out of the box every now and then and do something different."[8]

Stewart has unusual tastes. He has a pet iguana, tiger, and monkey, for example. The monkey's name is Mojo, and it loves Stewart. It once lunged at a large television because it was excited to see Stewart on TV competing in a race. It also pouts whenever Stewart leaves it at its Charlotte home.

In his mid-thirties, Stewart is still single. He has dated many women, but he has not settled down yet to get married. The hectic NASCAR schedule makes it difficult on him, he said.

"If the right person came along, I think he'd be happy to get married and have children. I think eventually he'd like to have a helpmate and someone to travel with," his mother said. "It's just that with his chaotic lifestyle right now, it's difficult to find the right person."[9]

Stewart is a very loyal person. He still keeps many of the same friends he had as a child and is close with his old neighbors and family. He also has worked with the same crew chief since he started in NASCAR: Greg Zipadelli. He wants to stay with Zipadelli as long as he is racing.

"We've been through the highest highs and lowest lows together," Stewart said. "That's what has kept us together for so long.

"I feel like he's a member of the family. I would be heartbroken if I couldn't drive for him."[10]

Stewart was recently voted the fourth-most popular driver in NASCAR. His popularity is due to many things: He wins, he is outgoing, he relates well to NASCAR fans, and he loves the sport. "Most people like him for who he is: fun, focused, and competitive," his mother said.[11]

He is so popular that he has a thriving fan club. His sister, Natalie Stewart, runs the club. When people call her to order souvenirs and start memberships in the club, she sometimes tells them stories of what the real Tony Stewart is like.

"Like when he used to tickle me until I'd cry or beat me up to sit in the front seat of the car," she said. "That's the Tony I know."[12]

Stewart is a tough driver. In 1996 he practiced for races while nursing severe injuries at home in Indianapolis. He had suffered multiple injuries in a Las Vegas accident earlier in the year. But he attacked his rehabilitation, rather than follow the methodical schedule that doctors had prepared for him. He had a friend lift him out of his wheelchair and into a go-kart every day. He would drive the go-kart around an indoor track for hours.

In 2006 Stewart won a race at Watkins Glen while driving with a nasty stomach flu and competed in another race with a broken shoulder blade.

"I'm a racecar driver, and that's all I've ever wanted to be," he said. "I didn't want that taken away from me."[13]

He won't be a racecar driver forever, though. He hopes to retire from NASCAR when he is still fairly young. Then he can spend more time managing Eldora, racing on dirt tracks, hanging with his friends and family, and maybe even running racing teams. He owns teams in the World of Outlaws and USAC racing series.

"At least this would be something for me to do," he said. "It gives me an option for something else to do the rest of my life if something happened."[14]

Of course, Stewart may end up racing in NASCAR for much longer than he or anybody else thinks is reasonable. "I might be one of those guys who wakes up one morning and says 'I've had enough' or decide to sign another five-year contract," he said. "You know me. It may depend on which way the wind's blowing."[15]

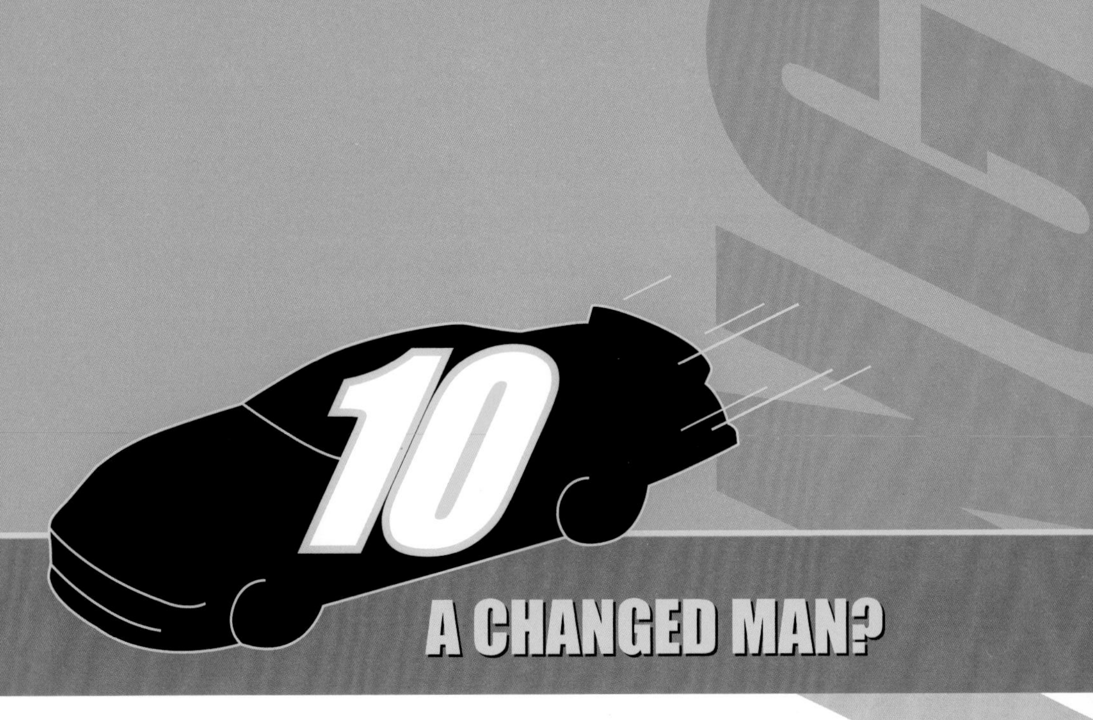

10 A CHANGED MAN?

After winning his second series championship on NASCAR's top circuit, Tony Stewart wanted to enjoy himself at the end of 2005 and beginning of 2006. He spent time with his friends and family, soaked up the glory with his team, and prepared for the 2006 season.

Yet, as soon as the year 2006 started, the problems began for Stewart. In January, he flipped his car during a qualifying race for the Chili Bowl Midget Nationals, an amateur race in Oklahoma that he had entered just for fun. Because of the wreck,

Stewart broke his wrist and bruised his ribs. He had to wear a cast on his arm for nearly a month.

That mishap slowed Stewart down to begin the 2006 Nextel Cup season, but it did not keep him out of any series races. He had the cast removed just in time for the season-opening race at Daytona, but then he had his customary slow start.

He finished last in the second race of the season, at California Speedway on February 26, and placed twenty-first in the next race at Las Vegas Motor Speedway on March 12. Those two races dropped the defending champion to nineteenth in the standings, but Stewart rallied.

The next week, he placed fifth in Atlanta. Then he won in Martinsville April 2, placed third the next week in Fort Worth, and finished second in the following two races at Phoenix and Talladega.

Stewart's impressive four-race run got him up to third in the series standings. He rose to second after placing sixth the next week at Richmond but then began to slide back. Stewart finished no higher than twelfth in any of the next three races, including a next-to-last finish at Charlotte May 28.

DIFFICULTIES ON THE TRACK

In the Charlotte Coca-Cola 600, Stewart crashed just thirty-two laps into the race. He suffered injuries so severe that he could not finish the race. The injuries also kept him from finishing the next week's race. In order to earn points from that race at Dover International Speedway, Stewart started as the driver of his Home Depot No. 20 car, but Ricky Rudd finished the race for him.

In pain, Stewart holds his arm as he is helped to an ambulance after a 2006 crash.

Stewart soon returned. But his troubles were not past. He placed forty-first at Michigan International Speedway on June 18 and twenty-eighth the next week at Infineon Raceway and fell to seventh in the series. He was quickly losing his grip on his title defense.

"We've been all over the board this season," Stewart said. "We had the best start to the season in my history in the series. . . . But it's not been a typical year for us, by any means."[1]

All Stewart could do at one point was to make fun of himself and the strange season he was having. "I was fully intending on sliding a Busch car on its roof at Talladega, breaking a shoulder blade, breaking ribs preseason, and bouncing up and down in the point standings," Stewart joked. "This is perfect—exactly where we wanted to be."[2]

Stewart could not stay down for long, though. He led the Pepsi 400 on July 1 for eighty-six laps

Stewart poses with the IROC trophy in Victory Lane on April 7, 2006.

and cruised to a second straight victory in that race at Daytona. That win moved Stewart back up to fifth in the standings. He celebrated by jumping into a crowd full of fans. He hoped that the victory would turn his season around.

It did not.

STEWART'S 2006 SEASON

Wins: Five

Place: Eleventh

Top-five finishes: Fifteen

Races not completed: Two

OUT OF THE CHASE

After the Daytona win, he had poor races at Chicagoland Speedway and New Hampshire International Speedway. He placed thirty-seventh at New Hampshire, sinking to eleventh in the standings.

Stewart was in a hole, but he refused to give up trying to defend his title. He finished in the top three in two straight races—at Watkins Glen International on August 14 and at Michigan on August 20.

Unfortunately, not even that hot stretch could help him qualify for the Chase for the Nextel Cup. After placing eighteenth at Richmond International Raceway on September 9, he fell into eleventh place in the series. Only ten races remained in the season. That meant that Stewart did not make the Chase for the first time since it had been instituted.

"We were devastated," Stewart said. "None of us would have dreamed we would be in a position where we would not be in the Chase."[3]

Stewart could not win a second straight Nextel Cup, because he was not one of the top ten drivers heading into the final ten races of the season. But he was the best driver during the Chase.

He kicked it off by placing second at New Hampshire on September 17, then won two weeks later at Kansas Speedway. He won in Kansas even though he had to run dry for the last half-lap, drifting across the finish line just head of his competitors.

He placed fourth at Martinsville Speedway on October 22 and then won the next week in Atlanta. He promptly won again the following week in Fort Worth. He was dominant in that race, the Dickie's 500, leading for 278 of 334 laps. It was the sixth time of the season that he paced the field in laps led.

"It was an awesome day," Stewart said. "Anytime you can lead that many laps in a race, it's a good day for you. Today was one of those days when we had a car that was good from start to finish.

"Last week was one of them and this week was another one of them, and it's few and far between where you can say that you've had cars that were this dominant. . . . We could get a straightaway lead at any time. I was loose the whole day, but we were extremely fast being loose."[4]

The wins in Atlanta and Texas gave Stewart three victories in six races. He led for 64 percent of the combined laps in those two races, winning consecutive races for the sixth time in his career.

"He's looking great," Earnhardt, Jr. said. "He has sort of rekindled his spirit a bit, I'd say."[5]

"In an injury-riddled season filled with missed opportunity," one columnist wrote, "Stewart still chose to make the most of his year."[6]

Stewart finished eleventh overall. He could not place higher than tenth despite his strong finish, because he was not in the ten-driver Chase. But with five wins, he posted the second-most victories of any driver during the season. He also won more times during the Chase than any other driver and paced the series with 1,360 laps led on the season.

He finished 2006 with an amazing ten victories in his previous fifty-seven races, dating back to 2005.

"This is why we'll be champions again," Stewart said. "Even though we didn't get in the Chase, we (did) a good job. . . . We're working hard at keeping our stats and everything up where we want them to be. It makes me feel good that we (did) a

IN THE LEAD

On October 29, Stewart won the 2006 Bass Pro Shops 500 in Atlanta. He led for 146 of the 325 laps.

good job this late in the season when we don't have a championship to run for."[7]

"The 2002 and 2005 series champion handled himself with extraordinary class after failing to make the Chase," a newspaper columnist wrote. "He promptly won three of 10 races. How's that for sending a message?"[8]

A NEW ROLE

Although Stewart could not defend his Nextel Cup title in 2006, he experienced a meaningful season. He became the elder statesman among drivers for Joe Gibbs Racing, taking on a mentoring role with young drivers Denny Hamlin and J.J. Yeley after Bobby Labonte left the team.

"I have a responsibility to make sure the other two guys are comfortable, where Bobby always made sure I was comfortable," Stewart said.[9]

Stewart worked well with the two younger drivers. They benefited one another in practices and at several races, including the Allstate 400 in August.

During a yellow flag at Lap 42 of that race, Yeley called for Stewart on his radio. Yeley was ahead of Stewart at the time but came up with a plan.

"Give me a couple laps, let it spread out, and I'll let you go," Yeley said.

Stewart's reply was just one example of the responsible, team-focused role that he had assumed by his eighth year on the Nextel Cup circuit.

"No problem, man," Stewart said. "Just take care of that (car). You've got a good run going. Don't get yourself in any compromising positions, and you're going to have a good day."[10]

"The biggest thing I've seen in Tony is his role in really becoming a leader and a mentor," said J.D. Gibbs, team president of Joe Gibbs Racing. "If you ask him questions, he gives you really good advice."[11]

BACK IN THE CHASE

Stewart's respite from the Chase for the Nextel Cup was short-lived. In 2007, he was back into top-12 form on the track, and continued to let his personality shine away from it.

He ended the season in sixth place overall after winning three races and recording 23 finishes in the top 10.

Stewart's season was packed with highs and lows. In the season-opening Daytona 500, a crash eliminated him from the race and he completed only 152 of the 202 laps. His forty-third place finish ended up being the worst of the season for Stewart.

In typical Stewart fashion, he didn't stay down long. He placed eighth, seventh and second in his next three races. After a string of five races in which he only cracked the top ten twice, he placed eighth, sixth and sixth. After a fortieth-place finish in the 13th race of the year, he ended fifth, third and sixth.

At midseason, Stewart began his victory march. He won three times in a four-week span in July and August. He worked his way from the back of the field each time. He won the USG Sheetrock 400 at Chicagoland Speedway on July 15. The victory ended a streak of 20 races without a win, the longest such streak since his rookie year.

But he wanted more. The next week, Stewart was back at his favorite racetrack in the world, Indianapolis Motor Speedway. He won for the second time there on a perfectly hot and sunny day.

"I wanted it to be hot. I wanted it to be sunny, to where the track would get a little slippery," Stewart said. "It just seems like when it starts getting slick, that's when we really excel at this place. When it's got a lot of grip, everyone's fast. It's just a matter of who hits the perfect setup. It just seems like when it gets slick, the setups Zippy gives me, my driving style, they match each other."[12]

After a sixth-place finish at the Pennsylvania 500, Stewart won the Centurion Boats at the Glen in New York. The final four races heading into the Chase brought impressive results also: tenth, fourth, thirteenth and second.

As Stewart was set to begin his run for a third Cup championship, he was all business. Going into the Chase for the Nextel Cup, Stewart was in third place. Of course, with all 12 drivers beginning with a virtually

Stewart arrives at a drivers' meeting before the start of the 2004 Sylvania 300.

equal number of points, Stewart was considered as much of threat to win the crown as anyone else.

"All these things like right now [doing a media session] are a total distraction to what I'm trying to accomplish the rest of the season and that's why I'm not going to do any more than I have to do until the end of the year," Stewart said. "My goal is to win the championship and focus on the things I have to focus on to get that done."[13]

Stewart began the Chase well enough, with a third and a ninth to sit in second place. But a thirty-ninth place finish at the Dodge Dealers 400 landed him in fourth place, and he never recovered. He ended up slipping back to sixth place in the final standings.

Heading into the 2008 season, Stewart was preparing for another big change. In August, Gibbs Racing decided to end its 16-year relationship with General Motors-manufactured cars and switch to Toyota. Stewart won his first Cup in a Pontiac and his second in a Chevrolet.

Will winning in a Toyota be a challenge for Stewart? Past history says yes, and that he'll meet that challenge head on.

CAREER ACHIEVEMENTS

- Won the NASCAR Winston/Nextel Cup series title in 2002 and 2005

- Won the IRL title in 1997

- Won four USAC titles, including the 1995 Triple Crown

- Won national titles in World Karting Association

- Named USAC Rookie of the Year in 1991

- Named IRL Rookie of the Year in 1996

CAREER STATISTICS

Year	Rank	Starts	Wins	Poles
2007	6	36	3	0
2006	11	36	5	0
2005	1	36	5	3
2004	6	36	2	0
2003	7	36	2	1
2002	1	36	3	2
2001	2	36	3	0
2000	6	34	6	2
1999	4	34	3	2

Top 5	Top 10	Earnings	Points
11	23	$6,396,750	6,242
15	19	$7,285,280	4,727
17	25	$6,987,530	6,533
10	19	$6,221,710	6,326
12	18	$5,227,500	4,549
15	21	$4,695,150	4,800
15	22	$3,493,040	4,763
12	23	$3,200,190	4,570
12	21	$2,615,226	4,774

CHAPTER NOTES

CHAPTER 1: A SPECTACULAR SEASON

1. Curt Cavin, "Back Home Again," *AutoWeek*, August 15, 2005.
2. Ibid.
3. "Tony Stewart Biography," *tonystewart.com*, September 18, 2007, <http://www.tonystewart.com/bio/>.
4. Al Pearce, "A New Man," *AutoWeek*, November 28, 2005.
5. Bill Saporito, "NASCAR's Driving Force," *Time Magazine*, November 14, 2005.
6. Joe Saraceno, "Ability? Yes," *USA TODAY*, Feb. 21, 2005.
7. Al Pearce, "From Last to First," *AutoWeek*, November 25, 2002.
8. Lars Anderson, "Weekend Wrecker," *Sports Illustrated*, August 9, 2004.
9. Steve Ballard, "Stewart staying true to himself," *The Indianapolis Star*, February 16, 2003.
10. Chris Jenkins, "Stewart reaches summit," *USA Today,* August 8, 2005.

CHAPTER 2: GROWING UP

1. Curt Cavin, "Back Home Again," *AutoWeek*, August 15, 2005.
2. Bob Kravitz, "A Hoosier kid's dream comes true," *The Indianapolis Star*, August 8, 2005.
3. "Tony Stewart Biography," *tonystewart.com*, September 18, 2007, <http://www.tonystewart.com/bio/>.
4. David Newton, "Stewart more than just a hero in his hometown," *NASCAR.com*, August 4, 2006.
5. "Tony Stewart Biography," *tonystewart.com*, September 18, 2007, <http://www.tonystewart.com/bio/>.
6. "Stewart's mom is master manager," *Team Press Release*, May 10, 2003.
7. B. Duane Cross, "It's Stewart's time to be outspoken ambassador," *CNNSI.com*, December 10, 2002.
8. Dave Van Dyck, "Stewart's Dream Is Coming True," *Chicago Sun-Times*, May 26, 1996.
9. Mark Bechtel, "SSSSmokin'!," *Sports Illustrated*, December 22, 1999.

CHAPTER 3: BECOMING A PROFESSIONAL DRIVER

1. Skip Wood, "Stewart ready to turn page," *USA Today*, July 23, 1998.
2. Liz Clarke, "Polesitter is a newcomer to Indy," *The Dallas Morning News*, May 25, 1996.
3. Wire Reports, "Stewart first to win 3 divisions same year," *St. Petersburg Times*, November 27, 1995.
4. Beth Tuschak, "Stewart's IRL skills impress many," *USA Today*, February 1, 1996.
5. Charley Hallman, "Stewart Fast Settles in at Indy," *St. Paul Pioneer Press*, May 26, 1996.
6. Liz Clarke, "Polesitter is a newcomer to Indy," *The Dallas Morning News*, May 25, 1996.
7. Brian Schmitz, "Stewart is Racing for Scotty," *Orlando Sentinel*, May 25, 1996.
8. Charley Hallman, "Stewart Fast Settles in at Indy," *St. Paul Pioneer Press*, May 26, 1996.
9. Elton Alexander, "Death, Practice Help Rookie Stewart Evolve," *Cleveland Plain Dealer*, May 26, 1996.
10. Charley Hallman, "Stewart Fast Settles in at Indy," *St. Paul Pioneer Press*, May 26, 1996.
11. Ibid.
12. Bill Saporito, "NASCAR's Driving Force," *Time Magazine*, November 14, 2005.
13. Ibid.
14. Ibid.
15. Curt Cavin, "A Racing State of Mind," *AutoWeek*, July 6, 1998.
16. David Poole and Marcia C. Smith, "Stewart Shows He Has GN Potential," *Charlotte Observer*, October 5, 1997.
17. Ibid.
18. Wire Services, "Stewart Expands Horizons," *San Jose Mercury News*, October 9, 1997.
19. Skip Wood, "Stewart ready to turn page," *USA Today*, July 23, 1998.

CHAPTER 4: MAKING A BIG SPLASH IN NASCAR

1. Robin Miller, "Stewart speeds to head of class," *The Indianapolis Star,* December 23, 1999.
2. Mark Bechtel, "SSSSmokin'!," *Sports Illustrated*, December 22, 1999.
3. Skip Wood, "Stewart ready to turn page," *USA Today*, July 23, 1998.
4. Mark Bechtel, "SSSSmokin'!," *Sports Illustrated*, December 22, 1999.
5. Steve Ballard, "Rookie Stewart a quick study," *USA Today*, April 9, 1999.
6. Ibid.
7. Robin Miller, "Stewart may be a NASCAR novice," *The Indianapolis Star*, September 16, 1999.
8. Ibid.
9. Ibid.

CHAPTER 5: HIGHS AND LOWS

1. Steve Ballard, "Stewart's run," *The Indianapolis Star*, November 18, 2002.
2. Steve Ballard, "NASCAR crowns Hoosier," *The Indianapolis Star*, November 18, 2002.
3. Steve Ballard, "Stewart's run," *The Indianapolis Star*, November 18, 2002.
4. Steve Ballard, "Stewart contains the fire within," *The Indianapolis Star*, April 27, 2002.
5. Bob Kravitz, "It's about time for Stewart to grow up," *The Indianapolis Star*, August 7, 2002.
6. Jeff MacGregor, "Road Rage," *Sports Illustrated*, October 21, 2002.
7. Steve Ballard, "Stewart's run," *The Indianapolis Star*, November 18, 2002.
8. Ibid.
9. Mark Bechtel, "Finishing Touch," *Sports Illustrated: Winston Cup 2002*, Winter 2002.
10. Al Pearce, "From Last to First," *AutoWeek*, November 25, 2002.

11. Steve Ballard, "Stewart staying true to himself," *The Indianapolis Star*, February 16, 2003.

12. Al Pearce, "From Last to First," *AutoWeek*, November 25, 2002.

13. Steve Ballard, "Stewart finds peace of mind," *The Indianapolis Star*, July 29, 2003.

14. Jeff MacGregor, "Road Rage," *Sports Illustrated*, October 21, 2002.

15. Chris Jenkins, "NASCAR's image may be in for a wild ride," *USA Today*, November 15, 2002.

16. Steve Ballard, "NASCAR crowns Hoosier," *The Indianapolis Star*, November 18, 2002.

17. Ibid.

CHAPTER 6: A CONTROVERSIAL STAR

1. Lars Anderson, "Weekend Wrecker," *Sports Illustrated*, August 9, 2004.

2. Donna Fellows, "He Wins Races, but Not Hearts," *The Ledger*.com, December 18, 2006.

3. Ibid.

4. Bill Saporito, "NASCAR's Driving Force," *Time Magazine*, November 14, 2005.

5. Tony Fabrizio, "Drivers Slam NASCAR's New Car," *The Tampa Tribune*, December 1, 2006.

6. Jeff MacGregor, "Road Rage," *Sports Illustrated*, October 21, 2002.

7. Chris Jenkins, "Taking stock," *USA Today*, February 12, 2003.

8. Steve Ballard, "Stewart staying true to himself," *The Indianapolis Star*, February 16, 2003.

9. Mark Bechtel, "Getting Hot," *Sports Illustrated*, December 6, 2000.

10. Lars Anderson, "Weekend Wrecker," *Sports Illustrated*, August 9, 2004.

11. Steve Ballard, "Out of his time," *The Indianapolis Star*, August 6, 2004.

12. Lars Anderson, "Weekend Wrecker," *Sports Illustrated*, August 9, 2004.

13. Ibid.

14. Ibid.

15. Gary Graves, "Stewart trying to show a cooler, kinder image," *USA Today*, August 3, 2001.

16. Steve Ballard, "Out of his time," *The Indianapolis Star,* August 6, 2004.

17. Chris Jenkins, "Taking stock," *USA Today*, February 12, 2003.

18. David Newton, "Stewart more than just a hero," *NASCAR.com*, August 4, 2006.

19. Chris Jenkins, "NASCAR's image may be in for a wild ride," *USA Today*, November 15, 2002.

20. "Stewart docked 25 points and fined for bad language," *nascar.com*, July 31, 2007, <http://www.nascar.com/2007/news/headlines/cup/07/31/tstewart.docked.points/index.html?eref=/rss/news/headlines/cup> (November 15, 2007).

CHAPTER 7: A GROWING MATURITY

1. Al Pearce, "A New Man," *AutoWeek*, November 28, 2005.

2. Steve Ballard, "Stewart finds peace of mind," *The Indianapolis Star*, July 29, 2003.

3. Lee Montgomery, "Stewart taking role as champion in stride," *CNNSI.com*, April 22, 2003.

4. Steve Ballard, "Tony's Award," *The Indianapolis Star*, November 21, 2005.

5. Bill Saporito, "NASCAR's Driving Force," *Time Magazine*, November 14, 2005.

6. Al Pearce, "A New Man," *AutoWeek*, November 28, 2005.

7. Lars Anderson, "Who Has Been the Most Disappointing?" Sports Illustrated, June 23, 2003.

8. Dave Rodman, "Despite woes, defending champ still fighting," *CNNSI.com*, June 7, 2003.

9. Lee Montgomery, "Stewart taking role as champion in stride," *CNNSI.com*, April 22, 2003.

10. Ibid.

11. Steve Ballard, "Tony's Award," *The Indianapolis Star*, November 21, 2005.

CHAPTER 8: PROVING HIMSELF A CHAMPION

1. "Stewart ends years of frustration," *Associated Press*, August 8, 2005.
2. Gary Graves, "Stewart basks in glory of 2nd title," *USA Today*, November 22, 2005.
3. Curt Cavin, "Stewart's surge has few peers," *The Indianapolis Star*, August 19, 2005.
4. Steve Ballard, "Tony's Award," *The Indianapolis Star*, November 21, 2005.
5. Gary Graves, "Stewart basks in glory of 2nd title," *USA Today*, November 22, 2005.
6. "Stewart ends years of frustration," *Associated Press*, August 8, 2005.
7. Steve Ballard, "Tony's Award," *The Indianapolis Star*, November 21, 2005.

CHAPTER 9: GIVING BACK

1. "Joe Gibbs Racing and KaBOOM! Join in National Effort," *Press Release*, June 23, 2005.
2. Stewart selected as finalist for USG award," *Press Release*, June 24, 2004.
3. Sean McClelland, "Moraine auto workers flock to Tony Stewart," *Dayton Daily News*, December 13, 2006.
4. Larry Edsall, "Paying It Forward," *AutoWeek*, April 24, 2006.
5. Steve Ballard, "Stewart, Zipadelli avoid 7-year itch," *The Indianapolis Star*, January 27, 2005.
6. Ibid.
7. "'Smoke' Web Site Offers Last-Minute Holiday Shopping Options," *TheIndyChannel.com*, December 22, 2006.
8. Sean McClelland, "Moraine auto workers flock to Tony Stewart," *Dayton Daily News*, December 13, 2006.
9. Steve Ballard, "Racing's antihero," *The Indianapolis Star*, August 2, 2006.
10. Steve Ballard, "Stewart, Zipadelli avoid 7-year itch," *The Indianapolis Star*, January 27, 2005.
11. Curt Cavin, "Selling Stewart a family venture," *The Indianapolis Star*, November 9, 2000.

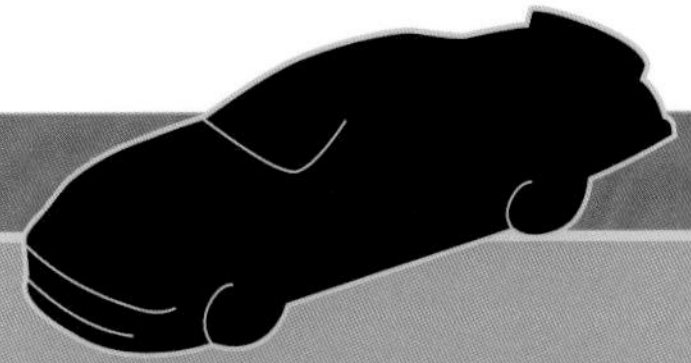

12. Ibid.

13. Curt Cavin, "A Racing State of Mind," *AutoWeek*, July 6, 1998.

14. Jenna Fryer, "Stewart already planning for life after racing," *The Associated Press*, February 24, 2005.

15. Ibid.

CHAPTER 10: A CHANGED MAN?

1. Dave Rodman, "Q&A: Tony Stewart: Champ looks to put bumpy road behind," *NASCAR.com*, June 24, 2006.

2. Ibid.

3. David Newton, "Chasers lucky Stewart didn't get fit sooner," *NASCAR.com*, November 6, 2006.

4. "Texas-Sized Dominance," *TonyStewart.com*, November 5, 2006.

5. David Newton, "Chasers lucky Stewart didn't get fit sooner," *NASCAR.com*, November 6, 2006.

6. Tom Bowles, "A year to remember," *SI.com*, December 19, 2006.

7. Gary Graves, "Stewart made most of missing chase," *USA Today*, November 22, 2006.

8. John Sturbin, "A look back at the best and worst," *Fort Worth Star-Telegram*, November 26, 2006.

9. Steve Ballard, "Stewart seen as voice of reason," *Indianapolis Star*, February 18, 2006.

10. Mark Alesia, "Stewart keeps his cool despite problems," *Indianapolis Star*, August 7, 2006.

11. Dave Rodman, "Conversation: J.D. Gibbs," *NASCAR.com*, June 21, 2006.

12. David Caraviello, "As the summer sun heats up, so does Stewart," *nascar.com*, July 30, 2007, <http://www.nascar.com/2007/news/headlines/cup/07/30/tstewart.indy.win/index.html> (November 15, 2007).

13. Dave Rodman, "Stewart focused on single goal in return to the Chase," *nascar.com*, September 15, 2007, <http://www.nascar.com/2007/news/headlines/cup/09/15/tstewart.dhamlin.loudon.chase/index.html> (November 15, 2007).

FOR MORE INFORMATION

ON THE WEB

Tony Stewart Fan Club:
http://www.tonystewartstore.com/fanclub.aspx

Joe Gibbs Racing: www.joegibbsracing.com

Tony Stewart Foundation: http://www.tonystewartfoundation.com/

FURTHER READING

Mitchell, Jason. *Tony Stewart: Driven To Win*. Chicago: Triumph Books, 2002.

Poole, David. *Tony Stewart: 2005 Nextel Cup Champion*. Chicago: Sports Publishing, 2005.

Stewart, Tony and Mark Bourcier. *True Speed: My Racing Life.* New York: Harper Paperbacks, 2003.

ON DVD

Tony Stewart—Smoke. Released in 2003 by Dreamworks.

GLOSSARY

Busch series—A NASCAR circuit featuring slightly lighter and less powerful cars with events generally run the day before Winston Cup (now Nextel Cup) races.

Chase for the Nextel Cup—Competition among the top ten drivers on the Nextel Cup series during the last ten races of the season. The winner is awarded the Nextel Cup.

crew chief—The person in charge of the driver's car.

drafting—When a driver moves close to another driver who is in front, to cut down on wind resistance.

go-karts—Small, four-wheel racecars that are open and low to the ground.

Indy cars—Open-wheeled racing cars with a single seats and a turbocharged rear engines.

IRL—Indy Racing League; a league of racing for Indy cars on oval tracks.

NASCAR—National Association for Stock Car Auto Racing.

Nextel Cup—The award given annually to the winner of NASCAR's top series.

quarter midget—Open-wheeled cars with one-fourth the size and power of a midget car, generally for younger competitors.

Rookie of the Year—The award given to the first-year NASCAR driver with the best fifteen finishes.

setup—The complete preparation of a car for a race.

sprint cars—Small, high-powered racecars designed to run mostly on short dirt and paved tracks.

stock cars—Racing cars that have a chassis similar to those of regular commercial cars and are about the same size.

team—All employees and staff of an organization assigned to a particular car.

USAC—United States Auto Club; an organization that oversees professional racing leagues for open-wheel drivers.

Victory Lane—A section of the track infield in which the winning car and team celebrate.

Winston Cup—The award given annually to the winner of NASCAR's top series from 1971 to 2003.

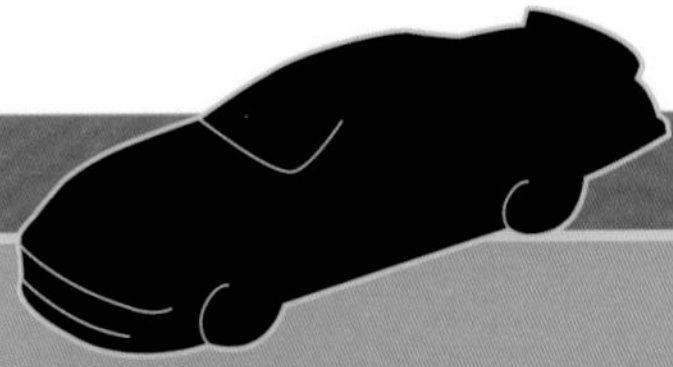

INDEX

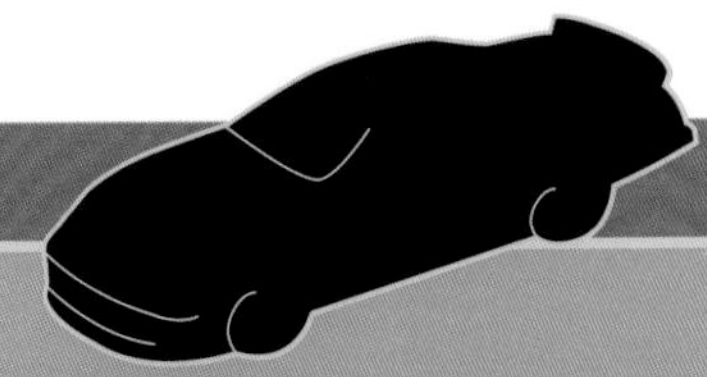

S

T

V

W

Y

Z